ROUTLEDGE LIBRARY EDITIONS: MANAGEMENT

Volume 31

ORGANIZATIONAL DESIGN FOR MARKETING FUTURES

ORGANIZATIONAL DESIGN FOR MARKETING FUTURES

ROY HAYHURST AND GORDON WILLS

LONDON AND NEW YORK

First published in 1972 by George Allen & Unwin Ltd

This edition first published in 2018
by Routledge
2 Park Square, Milton Park, Abingdon, Oxon OX14 4RN

and by Routledge
711 Third Avenue, New York, NY 10017

*Routledge is an imprint of the Taylor & Francis Group, an informa
business*

© 1972 George Allen & Unwin Ltd

All rights reserved. No part of this book may be reprinted or
reproduced or utilised in any form or by any electronic, mechanical,
or other means, now known or hereafter invented, including
photocopying and recording, or in any information storage or
retrieval system, without permission in writing from the publishers.

Trademark notice: Product or corporate names may be trademarks or
registered trademarks, and are used only for identification and
explanation without intent to infringe.

British Library Cataloguing in Publication Data
A catalogue record for this book is available from the British Library

ISBN: 978-1-138-55938-7 (Set)
ISBN: 978-1-351-05538-3 (Set) (ebk)
ISBN: 978-0-8153-7005-5 (Volume 31) (hbk)
ISBN: 978-1-351-25088-7 (Volume 31) (ebk)

Publisher's Note
The publisher has gone to great lengths to ensure the quality of this
reprint but points out that some imperfections in the original copies
may be apparent.

Disclaimer
The publisher has made every effort to trace copyright holders and
would welcome correspondence from those they have been unable to
trace.

ORGANIZATIONAL DESIGN FOR MARKETING FUTURES

ROY HAYHURST AND
GORDON WILLS

in association with

JAMES MANN PETER COOKE AND SADDIK SADDIK

London
GEORGE ALLEN AND UNWIN LTD
RUSKIN HOUSE MUSEUM STREET

First published in 1972

This book is copyright under the Berne Convention. All rights are reserved. Apart from any fair dealing for the purpose of private study, research, criticism or review, as permitted under the Copyright Act, 1956, no part of this publication may be reproduced, stored in a retrieval system, or transmitted, in any form or by any means, electronic, electrical, chemical, mechanical, optical, photocopying, recording or otherwise, without the prior permission of the copyright owner. Enquiries should be addressed to the publishers.

© George Allen & Unwin Ltd 1972

ISBN 0 04 658135 9

Printed in Great Britain
in 11pt Baskerville type
by Alden & Mowbray Ltd
at the Alden Press, Oxford

This book is dedicated to the scores of postgraduate students who have followed marketing courses at the University of Bradford Management Centre since 1965 and who have urged us to relate textbook normative theories to contemporary company practice; and in particular to those dozen or so who helped with the research chores involved in the series of investigations of which this book is the culmination.

CONTENTS

Introduction and Purpose   *page* 13

PART A MARKETING'S FUTURE TASKS – SOME
        SCENARIOS
A.1 The Corporate Planning Backlash   20
A.2 Problem Orientations   23
A.3 Social and Political Momentum   32
A.4 The Customer Backlash   36
A.5 Fashions and Fads   40

PART B HISTORICAL DEVELOPMENT OF MARKETING
        ORGANIZATIONS   45
B.1 Theory and Practice in Organization Structures 45
B.2 The Evolution of Marketing Structures   52
B.3 Structural Alternatives   56
     (a) Function Oriented   57
     (b) Product Oriented   59
     (c) Regionally Oriented   62
     (d) Customer-Type Orientation   63
     (e) Divisionalized Marketing Structures   64
B.4 The Organization of Marketing Subsystems   67
     (a) Sales Force Organization   67
     (b) Marketing Research Departments   69
     (c) Product Manager or Market Manager?   71
B.5 Some Emergent Principles   76
     (a) Analysis of Company Needs   79
     (b) Analysis of Human Needs   80
     (c) Structure from the Top   81
     (d) Proper Balance of Talent   82

10 CONTENTS

(e) Staffing with the Right People 83
(f) Design of Adequate Controls 83
(g) Built-in Co-ordination 84
(h) Evolution not Revolution 85
B.6 References cited in Part B 86

PART C BRITISH ORGANIZATIONAL STATUS QUO 89
C.1 Introduction 89
C.2 The Chief Marketing Executive and his
Responsibilities 92
C.3 The Marketing Department 98
C.4 External Agencies 102
C.5 Advertising and Promotion 103
C.6 Pricing 108
C.7 Distribution Channels 109
C.8 Sales Forecasting 110
C.9 Written Down Marketing Plans 111
C.10 Organizing for Marketing Research 114
(a) The Development of Marketing Research
in the United Kingdom 114
(b) The Current Status of Marketing Research 116
(c) Designation of Marketing Research
Executives 118
(d) Responsibility for Marketing Research
Executives 118
(e) Expenditure on Marketing Research 119
(f) Profile of Marketing Research Activities 121
C.11 Marketing Attitudes and Definitions 126

PART D ORGANIZATIONAL TRANSFER –
ORGANIZATIONAL DEVELOPMENT 135
D.1 The Routinization of Operational Marketing
Activities 135
D.2 The Fusion of Marketing Development and
Technical Research and Development 143
D.3 The Customer Service Function 149
D.4 Marketing Intelligence Systems 152
D.5 Total Distribution Approaches 157
D.6 The International Dimension 161

D.7	Ethics and Aesthetics	164
D.8	Educational Development and Training	167
D.9	The Present/Future Dichotomy in Organizational Design	171

APPENDIX 1	Research Methodology Employed in Survey of Companies	177
APPENDIX 2	Survey Questionnaires on the Marketing Organizational Status Quo	179
APPENDIX 3	Selection of Definitions of Marketing by Chief Marketing Executives	209
Index		211

INTRODUCTION AND PURPOSE

This book takes a deep and critical look at the way in which we organize the marketing activity of British industry. It reports on current practice in over 500 major British firms and as such provides a much needed bench mark for practising marketing executives. It is to over 100,000 such individuals that this book is addressed. Not only can companies now compare their own pattern of organization with what goes on in other businesses; they can view their own organization in a relevant perspective, and cull ideas and styles of activity that can then usefully be incorporated within their own operations.

Simultaneously, however, we have in mind two other vitally important target markets for this book. Firstly, we address our findings to the growing body of HND, undergraduate and postgraduate students, who have a desperate need for empirical data and information about British marketing activity both as a counterweight to the widespread dissemination of North American evidence and as an antidote to the textbook norms. Textbooks on marketing have had little to say about organization structures which are appropriate for the marketing activity in business and where they do pronounce it is normally only to regale the reader with a series of conventional charts – an approach which ignores the dynamics of organization structure and almost all the research findings about behaviour in organizations since the 1930s.

Secondly, we have borne in mind the needs so often expressed amongst general managers and amongst non-marketing specialists who come into contact with the marketing fraternity. These line managers and staff specialists frequently seek after a clearer understanding of marketing's task within the business in their efforts to develop both the overall and interacting aspects of

14 INTRODUCTION AND PURPOSE

the organization. For the many firms in industry who are not heavily committed to an established marketing activity this book can, and we hope will, act as a catalyst to ensure that a realistic and profitable understanding of how marketing can be deployed will emerge.

This book is essentially the outcome and culmination of a series of studies initiated at the University of Bradford Management Centre in 1966. We set out at that time to explore the extent to which manufacturing industry had accepted the marketing concept, the extent to which the customer had been placed first in the orientation of business strategies and policies. We began in a modest way with a small postal survey amongst 335 Yorkshire businessmen and the results were published, over James Mann's name, as *The Nominal and Effective Status of Chief Marketing Executives in Yorkshire Industry* in the Proceedings of Second Annual Conference of Marketing Teachers at an Advanced Level, 1967, pp. 70–80. The full results of that study appeared as a University of Bradford Management Centre Project Report, by M. Baker, T. Braam, and A. Kemp, *The Permeation of the Marketing Concept in Yorkshire Industry*, June 1967.

Dr Saddik began a more intensive study within three sectors of the British textile industry in 1967. He looked specifically at wool textiles, textile machinery and the clothing industries to examine the pattern of marketing organization and the extent to which the constituent firms were market oriented. His massive report, for which he received his doctorate, is published in two volumes, *Marketing in the Wool Textile, Textile Machinery and Clothing Industries*, 1969, and runs to nearly 1,000 pages. He examined 36 organizations in depth and followed up with a postal quantification study of 308 firms.

With both our widespread study of Yorkshire businessmen and Dr Saddik's in-depth investigation behind us, we felt ourselves ready to take a long look at British industry at large. The challenge implicit in any such study was enormous and we needed to avoid falling between the two stools representing substantial in-depth knowledge of just a few firms and a study of all British firms from the largest to the smallest at a superficial level.

As is indicated in some detail in Appendix 1, we determined

INTRODUCTION AND PURPOSE 15

to adopt a methodology similar to that evolved for Dr Saddik's examination of three textile sectors. We would look in depth at up to 100 firms with a semi-structured survey method and we would then quantify major dimensions by post with the totality of British industry with gross annual sales revenue of £¼ million or more in 1967. (This year was the latest for which the then Board of Trade had data conveniently available.) Such a research design was costly – in academic terms. We required not only to allocate our own staff time at Bradford over a considerable period of time but we also required petty cash for fieldwork expenses.

We are greatly indebted to the British Institute of Management for the help they provided in making a research grant to meet our cash outgoings. Their sponsorship, through the good offices of Dr John Marsh, BIM's Director-General, and Tom Cauter, then its Executive Director, made this study possible. In addition to financial aid, however, Tom Cauter and his colleagues contributed substantially to the structure of the investigation and this aid we also gratefully acknowledge.

If this book were merely to report the findings of our investigation we feel it would be a valuable addition to our knowledge. However, we have sought to go considerably further than just making a formal report. Organizations are dynamic, living systems. They have been described in ecological terminology as sentient ecosystems. To take just a single snapshot of British marketing organization in 1968/9 and to report on it in 1972 would, we felt, be to half complete our task.

In this book we have accordingly placed our findings in the context of a simple dynamic model of the purpose of marketing organizations. We postulate that organizations in the marketing field are established to accomplish a marketing task through a given structure, and that as the tasks and/or the individuals within the structure change, so must the total pattern of organization.

To help ensure that British industry in the decade ahead has the right pattern of marketing organization we have felt it appropriate to identify what the marketing tasks are likely to be during the next decade or so. We have written scenarios of that next decade and offer them as the environment in which the individual corporate marketing task must be undertaken. These

16 INTRODUCTION AND PURPOSE

appear as Part A of this book. In Part B we have taken a look at the evolution of conceptual and intellectual thought about the nature of marketing's task and the organization of business activities in general. In particular, we review theories of organization and what research has so far discerned. This Part has been particularly assisted by the work of James Mann and Peter Cooke, colleagues at The Management Centre, who were involved in several aspects of this project. Peter Cooke in particular prepared much of an early draft of Part B.

Part C contains the full gamut of our findings in our empirical study and sets the stage for our attempt in Part D to identify the directions of organizational development which will be fundamental to the accomplishment of the future marketing tasks we have identified in Part A. Part D we have entitled Organizational Transfer to highlight the transition from the organizational *status quo* described in Part C.

Hence, our overall purpose has been to demonstrate how the present pattern of marketing organization in British industry is just a stepping stone between earlier historical concepts and the structure we need for the decade ahead. It is our hope that, by structuring the book in the dynamic framework which we have adopted, we can focus the attention of our identified market on the need for a consciously organic approach towards the development of marketing organization.

Our theme is not new. For the conceptual orientation of much which has emerged in Part D, we have our Bradford academic colleague Chas Margerison to thank. He is, of course, not responsible for what we suggest, but he has been tireless in his efforts to convert us and all he meets in industry to the movement towards a more coherent policy of organizational development in each and every sector of British industry and within each and every functional or specialist area of activity of the firm.

We are equally indebted to Saddik Saddik for help at several stages of this study. Although Dr Saddik had not fully completed his own investigation when this study began he was a tower of strength both in terms of the logistics of the investigation and as an adviser on methodology. He co-ordinated the initial stages of data evaluation before he was appointed as Lecturer in Marketing Studies at Liverpool University School

INTRODUCTION AND PURPOSE

of Business. Unfortunately, before he could take up that post he had to return, for family reasons, to Egypt where he is now lecturing in Marketing.

Secretarial and clerical assistance was efficiently provided by Heather McCallum, Anne Randle, Anne Collinson and Helga Werwie at various stages and to each of these we express our thanks.

Management Centre
University of Bradford

Roy Hayhurst
Gordon Wills

PART A

MARKETING'S FUTURE TASKS – SOME SCENARIOS

At the outset of our consideration of marketing organizational design, we shall identify what the future seems likely to hold in store for marketing activity within the business. We intend to do this through a series of probes into the future. These probes are made under five sub-headings – the corporate planning backlash, problem orientations, social and political momentum, the customer backlash, and fashions and fads.

Each probe involves a description of marketing organizational changes which can either be extrapolated from present trends or which a consensus of marketing experts has felt to be normatively worthwhile to identify.

The purpose of these probes, these scenarios, is to indicate the order of situations with which marketing will have to deal during the decades ahead. These represent the nature of the challenges to be faced and the opportunities to be made use of. Through normative statements of this type we believe it is more feasible both to plan the futures that our companies may wish to see and to cope with the futures with which we find ourselves confronted from time to time.

These scenarios are not simply pipe dreams of the authors. They have been developed in discussions with many of our colleagues at the Management Centre in the University of Bradford; with managers and students on our Bradford programmes; marketing executives at the ITT–Cannon Ball in Palma de Mallorca; participants at Institute of Marketing seminars, and academics at the Committee for Marketing Teachers' Second Marketing Theory Seminar at Ashridge Management College in March, 1969. They are accordingly not 'all our own work' although we are undoubtedly solely responsible for any errors.

20 ORGANIZATIONAL DESIGN FOR MARKETING FUTURES

Such scenario writing is a highly risky enterprise. What we have to describe will surely provoke our readers, and we shall undoubtedly make predictions with which a reader cannot concur. That is the nature of the exercise, and we do not view such dissent as a failure on our part. If we can act here as a catalyst to thought we shall be delighted.

A.I. THE CORPORATE PLANNING BACKLASH

The reassertion of natural corporate rights is perhaps the most powerful influence to which marketing organizations will need to adapt during the coming decade. These rights can be expected to make themselves manifest not primarily via a tighter grip of day-to-day operations in business but through a positive approach to medium- and long-term planning. Whilst this phenomenon can be characterized as ironic, it has, throughout, seemed virtually inevitable. The irony, of course, arises from consideration of the conception, gestation and birth of the planning function in most businesses. Planning was normally engendered during the adolescence of customer-based research investigations and marketing planning. Yet it was such early success which generally caused marketeers to overstep themselves. The smack of hard facts which characterizes the 'survey power' of the marketing executive and his information farmers has and will continue to prove unanswerable in the shorter-term business situation.

But in the middle and long distance the customer's voice consistently grows less distinct. Product concepts, future price possibilities and hypothetical channels of distribution can only be subjected to testing at a low level of sophistication, with a poor cost/benefit outcome. The middle- and long-distance strategic ground of business leaves the marketing executive exposed. He cannot embrace the rapid developments in technological, sociological and cultural forecasting. There is such a high level of noise on his direct line to the customer it is unable to continue to serve as a basis for corporate authority. Financial and production managements implicitly and intuitively are already seizing their opportunity to reassert the eternal truth of corporate purpose – 'to deploy all possible resources in the service of corporate objectives by the exploitation of customer needs'.

MARKETING'S FUTURE TASKS – SOME SCENARIOS 21

Marketing too has probably overstretched its span of control. By seeking to take up the middle ground it has sought to pre-empt the initiative of others in corporate diversification, new product introduction, and licensing arrangements. Its concepts of product strategy based on philosophic disputations about the market, may well lead first to the neglect of its own operational task and then to its amputation. In essence, it is likely to become apparent that whilst in its early days it had been natural to accept marketing as the locus of planning to determine the future pattern of corporate activity, almost inevitably such a devolution of planning will lead to disequilibrium in the pursuit of corporate objectives. Hence, marketing in the seventies must be confronted with two diverging strands of planning activity – the first for operational activity designed to meet short-term corporate objectives, which must remain the true bailiwick of marketing as a programmed activity. The second will increasingly look at those planning aspects which will determine the future development of the corporate activity. This latter planning activity, which will emerge mainly from within the marketing womb, will grow away from the programmed activity into a discrete concern with the future. It will search for opportunities both for creating a part of that future, and forecasting what would occur in those sectors it did not seek to create.

This potential divorce of the short- from medium- and long-term facets of contemporary marketing activity is nowhere more clearly demonstrated than in the emerging pattern within the conglomerate and holding company. The conglomerate business exemplifies the re-emergence of the financial function in business as the controller of its corporate destiny, an ascendancy that has occurred largely at the expense of the customer orientation championed by the marketing function and its concomitant philosophical concepts. The conglomerate operates predominantly in terms of a complete abdication of *first order* corporate concern with the customers, or markets, or their segmentation. It works to meet, for example, required rates of return on capital employed. Certainly the criteria are financial ratios of one sort or another. Markets and customers became a *second order* consideration as the means to that required financial ratio. The logic of range analysis or diversification does not follow the direction of Levitt enshrined in 'Marketing Myopia' and the

22 ORGANIZATIONAL DESIGN FOR MARKETING FUTURES

'what market are we in? catalyst' to our thoughts. Resources are increasingly, perhaps inevitably, made available as between units or divisions of a conglomerate or holding company in terms of forecast financial returns and not on the basis of product market strategies. Simultaneous with the exposure of 'survey power' as a weak instrument for medium- and long-distance planning of corporate activities, marketing organization will be increasingly influenced by the harnessing of computer power to the problems of short-term planning and control in business situations. Even in that area where the professional competence of the marketing executive is currently accepted as uniquely valid, the development of computer systems will soon enable senior, corporate management to retract some of the responsibilities for planning and control which early complexities, unharnessed to computer power, had made insoluble at a central focus. This pincer movement, squeezing the medium/long term, and the shorter-term facets of conventional marketing organizational roles will create a traumatic experience. The emergence of such a sophisticated computer technology will demand the revision of Graicunas' original span concepts of control for the organization. The single or small firm entrepreneurial role can soon be reinstated in all save the most complex companies and even here further major advances in computer technology can confidently be expected. The survey data's range of alternative interpretations will be simulatable and possible outcomes will be explorable. The value of the intuitive best judgement of the professional will be circumscribed and the short-term task made yet more mechanical than hitherto. The residual discretion for the professional marketing job will become even more sharply focused on the specification of data to be collected and used as machine input.

Hence computer power will enable the individual entrepreneur to cope with an immensely greater range of corporate activities and to integrate and co-ordinate them effectively. Educationally, also, as a result of continuing advances in managerial training and education, the entrepreneurial function at the more sophisticated level within all areas will come within the intellectual grasp of many more of the individuals concerned. The co-ordination, for example, of data on investment appraisals, technological forecasts, customer behaviour, patterns of diffusion of analogous innovations will soon be within the scope of our computer technology and its corporate model; and within the comprehension of our corporate chief executive.

The corporate planning backlash against marketing's contemporary dominance of corporate philosophies will be brutal. It will quite simply demand the relegation of marketing to a programming role in precisely the same manner as the production function was relegated in the middle of this century. Associated with this mechanization will come a focusing of attention on the auditing of marketing activities and the improvement of their productivity. Work study and quality control sections will appear within the programmed marketing area akin to those already in programmed production. The policy-formulating role in the middle and long distance will be returned to the central corporate focus around the chief executive from whom it has been effectively, albeit unknowingly, usurped during the past several decades. Not only will the centre now be better equipped to cope because of the increased sophistication of management technology and planning procedures partly fostered during marketing's heyday, but also because of the increasing scope of management education. Advanced computer power will also make its vital contribution at the centre of the organization in facilitating the co-ordinating role and the necessity for delegated functions.

A.2. PROBLEM ORIENTATIONS

Marketing came to the fore in business organizations in Britain in the late fifties. Senior executives, steeped in their own professionalism as accountants or engineers had seen their companies faltering in the face of the onslaught from North American and German competitors. There was no doubt whatever at that time that a problem existed at the customer/business interface. Particularly in the mass markets where products sold to up to 50 million domestic customers and to countless potential customers beyond the ports, communications had broken down. Vast expenditures on advertising, totalling over £500 million per year in the sixties were frequently seen as acts of faith, but nonetheless, an inevitable necessity if contact with customers

24 ORGANIZATIONAL DESIGN FOR MARKETING FUTURES

was to be maintained. Simultaneously, the growth of marketing research enabled the customers' views to be known at the points of production and distribution of goods and services in a way more reminiscent of the craftsman of the Middle Ages when custom-building dominated the pattern of demand and supply.

The application of the insights of behavioural science – those of sociology and psychology, of anthropology and geography as well as those of economics – allied to the advances in quantitative techniques, has already begun to take the sting from this management problem during the late sixties and will increasingly do so. Reference group approaches, motivation research, diffusion theory, aspiration theory and a dozen more approaches have already shown their value both in reducing the problems posed and in enhancing the professionalism of marketing management. The extroverted self-confidence of the marketing function – the result, largely, of its early staffing by sales personnel – will give way to a more objective, reasoned approach to the planning and programming of marketing activities. Three major problems, however, will rear their heads and preoccupy senior executives in the way marketing has done so only recently. They are the problems of coming to terms with accelerating technological change in many sectors of the economy; adapting to a new international and European context in the conceptualization of market areas as well as in financial terms; and coping with 'seizures' in many channels of distribution. This latter area incorporating the twin challenges of physical logistics and channel structures is for Britain an essentially new phenomenon. The other two are surely fresh manifestations of problems which began to receive attention during the late fifties and sixties.

Arch Shaw had launched the marketing movement in the United States in 1912 with observations on the productivity of our marketing systems. Writing before the impact of the internal combustion engine, he commented:

'The most pressing problem for the businessman today is to study distribution systematically, as production is being studied. He must apply to his problems the methods of investigation that have proven of use in more highly developed fields of knowledge . . .' (*Some Problems of Distribution,* Harvard University Press.)

Shaw had referred to the discrepancy between the application of the work of the Gilbreths and Taylor to production and its absence in marketing. The techniques were predominantly from work study. In the seventies the discrepancy will lie between the application of the sophisticated procedures of operational research developed again primarily for and within the production function. Many of the techniques are capable of direct translation from the company manufacturing area, to be applied to stocks and their service levels in the distributive channels. Others, in terms of the optimum shelf allocation for retailers or wholesalers amongst 17,000 separate items will demand extensions of technique. Overall, however, will hang the problem of excess supply of like goods and services and their competitive differentiation in psychological terms rather than inherent product quality. This will lead to a perplexing growth in the number of virtually identical products and a sustained attempt to create customer brand insistence through massive promotional activity.

When allied to the probable major rationalization of distributive outlets catalysed by the abolition of resale price maintenance in the mid-sixties, this will inevitably lead to the growth of yet larger distributive units and multiple organizations with a concomitant growth of 'own-branding'. Indeed 'own-brands' will become a major force in many more sectors of consumer goods trades where product differentiation will become the major element in sterile corporate marketing activity. This trend will lead to a major switch in the proportional allocation of promotional effort between above- and below-the-line and as between manufacturer and distributor. Below-the-line activity will continue to escalate throughout the seventies and will increasingly originate from in-channel sources rather than from manufacturers. The focus of a manufacturer's promotion will switch in many sectors from the final customer to the intermediate who selected his supplier for his 'own-branded' products from a wide range of alternates.

The abolition of resale price maintenance was, of course, initially of most dramatic influence in grocery and other low-

26 ORGANIZATIONAL DESIGN FOR MARKETING FUTURES

value, fast-turnover goods and in more durable consumer goods. In the industrial sector, channels and marketing effort will also be brought into a finer, sharper focus. In particular, the optimum locations of warehousing and growth of service elements in many advanced technology products will bring major rationalization in channels and the flow of goods through them. The stock and service levels of intermediate distributors will improve substantially with the application of standard marketing research techniques on a continuous basis, borrowed from the consumer goods areas, for example the wholesaler audit and trade panel methods can be expected to become widely used.

This effort in the distribution sector of business will be demanded by the 'law of the situation'. Channels of distribution and the pattern of the movement of goods are becoming dramatically less and less efficient in the face of the massive increase in volume throughput. The automation of most warehousing and the use of advanced computer techniques in the linking of distributor orders direct to warehouse and thence to production point can become more widespread. The only check to this advance will come from the resurgence of public warehousing in the United Kingdom. How the advantages of the public warehouse have come to be ignored remains a mystery to this day, but in the early seventies a wave of warehousing centres will be opened in all the major areas of economic activity in the country. In these warehouses the best management organization will be available and linked via automation to computer scheduling of both deliveries inwards and outwards. Manufacturers, large and small, will frequently find the sub-contracting of this particular aspect of their business and the scheduling of local deliveries to outlets economically well worth while. Arguments about optimum warehouse location for the individual company will be replaced by complex decisions on the extent of warehousing 'peak stock' shedding. The initiative for many of these public warehouse schemes can be seen as coming from former wharf-owners in the over-congested docks. For their business, the advantage of storage near the water has been receding throughout the century. When the road system received its great fillip in the sixties, with the construction of nearly a thousand miles of motorway, the economic logic of expensive, congested, town centre warehousing went. This whole episode will be contemporaneous with the accelerating containerization revolution which will further facilitate the devolution of storage areas.

The accelerating rate of change in the technologies on which particular industries are based is already a common phenomenon, although in no way of equal concern to all. Those sectors which had experienced the most rapid change in the fifties, for example electronics, airframes and aeroengines, may well be followed in the seventies by food processing in particular as the world hunger problem and accelerating population growth are tackled.

The structure of Britain's trade has also been transformed from one predominantly based with the less developed countries to one based on trade with advanced industrial economies. This trend has, of course, emerged as a result of much of the planning of the early sixties and in response to the decline of many traditional sectors. The implications for marketing will come predominantly in the sectors attending to new product development and introduction. This group will ever be faced with a wider and wider range of alternative opportunities with increasingly high risks, not often in terms of conventional investment costs for plant or equipment, but in terms of market investment. In the increasing clamour of the market and the overloading of channels of distribution, the cost of entry and penetration of markets will often become prohibitive. Many new product introductions, both in consumer and industrial sectors, will come to be made on the basis of widespread 'sampling'. From machine tools to detergents, from washing machines to nuclear power stations, installations will increasingly be made on a sale-or-return basis over a relevant trial period. To gain conventional access to the customer through regular channels of distribution will often prove to be even more expensive. Naturally, sampling in high-value items will be most carefully carried out after a detailed evaluation of the critical influences of diffusion of new products into a society. Allied to word-of-mouth communications networks which will also be extensively charted, the cost effectiveness of such promotional activity may well prove to be quite startling.

The high cost of market penetration will be accompanied by

28   ORGANIZATIONAL DESIGN FOR MARKETING FUTURES

an escalation of the risk as well, and of the complexity inherent in evaluating alternative possible offerings. This will bring marketing into much greater contact with financial executives than hitherto. The accuracy of assessments of life cycles of various new technology products and the likely level of competitive retaliation will become critical in the financial planning of the business. Marketing will no longer be called upon to provide single point sales forecasts for products, but rather a range of possible levels of sales and probabilities of their outcome for sensitivity analysis by the financial experts.

Collaboration with the financiers will be paralleled at the interface with research and development in most companies. The growth of task forces and comprehensive venture analysis forecast during the sixties will come about in almost all industries as the only way of telescoping the process of successful development and market introduction of new products. The communications problems and organizational and professional inertia, first between the researcher and the engineer and then between the engineer and the marketing executive, will be broken down by a range of expedients ranging from the establishment of separate companies responsible for all stages of new product introduction until it can be handed over to an operational company to the use of the lone individual with full responsibility across all functions within the main organization.

Technological forecasting will come to pervade over the whole scene as more effective techniques are developed. Indeed, the positive emphasis associated with marketing will be translated to technological forecasting, giving particular emphasis to its normative approaches. Extrapolative methods, which were transferred directly in the first instance from sales forecasting, will give way very quickly with encouragement from both government and society at large to a purposeful planning of technology in the service of society's needs and in face of its problems. Galbraith's views on the technostructure and its dominance in the shaping of our society will prove sufficiently powerful for their worst consequences to be avoided. The preparation of scenarios and the use of the delphi method to gain the consensus of experts will become a regular facet of planning, hand-in-hand with the competitive mapping of technological development in competitive organizations.

MARKETING'S FUTURE TASKS – SOME SCENARIOS

For British companies of course the seventies will see many of the rewards reaped from the establishment of a coherent national policy for technology, through Mintech, in the sixties. The crucially significant restructuring of traditional British industries and the identification of priorities in specific sectors of high technology will begin to pay off. In major fields such as aeroengines, computers and nuclear power, Britain will take the lead in the European technological community, and although North American dominance will continue unabated in space technology, European technology will become fiercely competitive in a list of new sectors. The unavoidable decay of Britain's traditional industries such as cotton textiles, shipbuilding and coal will be accepted and from their assisted decline can arise realistic specialized successor industries, based on advanced technology. In this way, British industry will be able to leave behind the apparently insuperable problems of the sixties in terms of the international competitiveness of its products.

Credit for much of the success of this dramatic reorientation of British industry can be claimed for the reforms and planning activities of the Labour Reform Government under Harold Wilson, 1964–70. The work of Mintech was not unique. The National Economic Development Office and the Department of Economic Affairs, along with regional devolution and planning, industrial retraining, the mushroom growth of management education and of industrial training; the new coherence in industrial relations allied to the Prices and Incomes Policy; redundancy payment schemes and increased unemployment benefits; the stimulation of lower cost investment outside the congested industrial areas; the Industrial Reorganization Corporation, with its crucial role for restructuring over-diversified units and conglomerates; the EDC import/export studies by industry with their focus for action – all these gave a new dynamic to British industry at a time when the international life cycle found the American, Japanese and West German economies at a flabby stage and at a time of relatively declining growth.

As balance of payments problems have, in the sixties, hovered over the whole pattern of monetary activity and blinded many contemporary observers to the fundamental transformation

30 ORGANIZATIONAL DESIGN FOR MARKETING FUTURES

taking place, so the rebuffs from Gaullist France during its dominant decade have often led to a misreading of Britain's involvement with the European concept and its commitment to be an equal partner with an international, even supra-national, philosophy. The conversion, in the late sixties, of the British Labour Party to the European ideal meant that it was only a matter of time before Britain would join, and with the resignation of de Gaulle at the end of the decade, it became apparent just what had been achieved even from without. A European technological ideal has grown up despite the Gaullist resistance, and the tradition of tariff reform implicit in the European Free Trade Area is in the spirit of the times. Decimalization has been accepted more than a century after it was first seriously mooted, both in monetary terms, and for weights and measures of value and distance.

Most significantly, however, the series of vetoes imposed on British applications to join the European Economic Communities during the fifties and mid-sixties has psychologically prepared British industry for the eventuality. Despite the well-foreseen early problem of food prices, the competitiveness of British goods and services will be heartening, as will the competence of their distribution and marketing.

British experience in trading across the seas has its roots back through the centuries; certainly, it was a major factor in the sixteenth century. The integration of the six countries and the major EFTA members into a European economic union will give even greater power to the whole Western European economy to compete internationally in a way which even the diversity of the United States will be unable to match. Experience of multi-nation trading will come rapidly in its wake. The cultural problems which the North American executive has always had in the management of off-shore operations will become an even more exposed Achilles heel than has appeared the case in less united days for Europe.

The problems of international business outside of Britain, however, will remain far from resolved. Perhaps there can be no final solution since the changing cultural and political patterns in different countries continually undermine any currently effective formula. Nonetheless, the dominant trend will be toward the identification and classification of market segments,

Marketing's Future Tasks – Some Scenarios 31

regardless of national boundaries or custom posts, as the focus for marketing activities. The study of comparative marketing systems and the use of cluster analysis procedures for taxonomies of segments will prove particularly fruitful. The geographic location of head offices, although often of political significance, will become of less importance as air travel and indeed space travel shorten distances between one location and the other. Financial arrangements will still prove of considerable difficulty, but as with trade through the ages, the demands of effective interchange of goods will lead to an increasing degree of co-operation between countries in matters of law and money.

The focus of top management concern with various problems during the seventies will be on physical distribution in terms of channel structures and logistics; on the accelerating rate of technological change; and on the problems of international business, both in the European community and beyond. In each of these sectors, as has been the case with the customer/manufacturer communications breakdown of the fifties and sixties, satisfactory outcomes will emerge. British management will rise to meet the situation, in part because of the realistic groundwork of planning undertaken in the sixties and in part due to the increased skills brought to bear, particularly the advances in management education and industrial training and relationships.

The scope of many of marketing's conventional organizational points of reference will crumble, however. The points of contact with finance and research and development will lead to a wide variety of new organizational forms for marketing to attempt to enhance effectiveness in rapidly changing circumstances such as product innovation.

International business problems will lead to the abandonment of the domestic/export dichotomy in organization structures and the structuring of operations to meet the needs of all like customers wherever they may be located geographically. At the same time, however, it will lead to a greater degree of sensitivity to both the distinctive patterns of different cultures and the worthiness of preserving what is treasured in such cultures.

The physical distribution problem is, however, likely to be

32 ORGANIZATIONAL DESIGN FOR MARKETING FUTURES

the dominant preoccupation for managements in many industries. The solutions and outcomes of a host of diverse initiatives in logistics planning and the evolution of new channels for the movement of goods and provision of services will keep the problem at bay, and restore a substantial degree of efficacy to this area of corporate activity in line with the levels achieved in production aspects of the business in the sixties.

A.3. SOCIAL AND POLITICAL MOMENTUM

The impact of social, political and macro-economic factors on the pattern of marketing is at all times most hazardous to assess. Hindsight often lends such a simple explanation to the pattern of evolution in the business environment that it is difficult to understand why contemporary managements seemingly ignored it. Such, however, is the nature of those external variables which are partly created by the aggregated behaviour of all businesses and partly shaped by the ideals that inspire the political and social leaders of the day.

The dominant influence of the decade ahead must surely be a search for the equilibrium in social relationships which we lost in the sixties. Individualistic self-expression, with its direct implications for mass marketing and segmentation, will cease to be the violent preoccupation of the young, high-spending groups. This will be manifest on the political scene by a widening breach between the trade unions and the party of the left, and the emergence of two major central movements uninterested in either the far left or right in politics. In reference group terms, the decade can be discerned as a constant effort by inferiors to be assimilated with superiors and a constant effort by superiors to differentiate themselves; but not as individuals, rather as a new social elite based on taste, particularly in design.

Marketing segmentation approaches will supersede mass marketing in a wide range of business sectors, and in some a return to custom building by craftsmen will reflect the spirit of the times. This trend, of course, applies especially to conspicuous consumer goods – durables and the like – but also extends into industrial sectors in a quite surprising way. In essence, of course, this increased emphasis on personal or reference group satisfaction from goods and services will act as a counterweight to the increasing mechanization of so many aspects of the business and the exclusion of more and more from direct participation in top decision-making. The pattern of job satisfactions will change and of course, as time spent at work changes, so will the areas where satisfaction may be gained. Leisure pursuits and family involvement will take on much greater importance for the executive and the workforce. The former's hours of work have been increasing steadily for several decades until in the late sixties it became possible for almost all successful middle and senior management to be working a sixty to sixty-five hour week in comparison with forty hours for the workforce.

These general facets of the cultural and political environment in Britain will be made possible by a continued and indeed accelerating growth in disposable income per household at the same time as hours worked goes into its decline. The concept of disposable income may need further clarification for the marketing man. The proportion of such incomes which households allocate to fixed expenditures – such as mortgages or rent and to credit payments – affects the discretion which remains in their hands to satisfy individual or familial needs. Discretionary incomes as such will grow as a proportion of total incomes during the coming decade, due to the changing pattern of values in the British culture. One special way in which many will wish to spend substantial parts of their discretionary incomes is on forms of personal service long since forgotten in British society, and analogous in many ways to the propensity to opt for custom building in many product fields. The search for service, and the initial decline in its availability, will nowhere be more intense than in the distributive trades. There, the remorseless trend of the sixties towards the depersonalization of the retail trades particularly through supermarketing and discount trading, will be partially reversed. Mail order's personalized sales approach based in Britain, though not elsewhere, on the small social group established by an agent, has already heralded this trend during the sixties. But few have spotted it. In the seventies it will spread not solely in terms of a massive extension of mail order but in terms of a reconstruction of the retailing sector of the economy. Outlets such as home

34 ORGANIZATIONAL DESIGN FOR MARKETING FUTURES

furnishers, men's tailors, grocers, butchers (although they have never fully succumbed to the self-service trend) and garages will all develop retailing-into-the-home. The systems employed will vary widely from the reappearance of van-selling at the door to the use of telephone selling and order taking followed by delivery. The in-home sales situation will quickly conquer the tawdry image of doorstep selling so common for household utensils, encyclopaedias and insurance by the introduction of an appointments system. Even the GP who had taken to ever less frequently offering his services to the sick will find it is worth his while to call on his patients again! Bank managers also will join the movement and reopen on Saturdays.

To the student of 'the wheel of retailing' as the cycle had been dubbed in the fifties, this reversal of self-service/economy preferences in the distributive trades will not come as a surprise. It will, however, startle many who have made very substantial investment in out-of-town shopping centres in Britain in imitation of the North American trend.

Possibly the most important error of calculation made comes from a misinterpretation of the psychological and motivational studies of the housewife in the fifties and early sixties. These had indicated, all too clearly and correctly at the time, that for the housebound mother in the high consumption age groups, the shopping experience was one of the major social highlights of her life. The transformation of the educational scene in the sixties, however, outdated this evidence. As the classic calamitous instance of marketing research in the fifties for the US Ford Motor Company's Edsel car had demonstrated, consumer's tastes and motivations change.

Pre-school nurseries will become an almost universal phenomenon and this, allied to the increase in the school leaving age first to 17 and then to 18 and to the phenomenal growth of the Open University, will completely transform the social life of the married woman. Not only will she be freed from restrictive ties but she will rapidly become of significant importance in the service economy on a part-time basis. This trend has already been dramatically brought to public attention with the introduction of the selective employment tax covering, particularly, the distributive trades under the Wilson Reform Government of the sixties. That tax had initially penalized the service sector of

MARKETING'S FUTURE TASKS – SOME SCENARIOS 35

the economy, particularly distributive trades, in order to favour productive economic activities. This was, however, a last gasp of the Marxist doctrine that distribution costs were parasitic. Costs of distribution in the economy will in fact rise quite substantially during the coming decade as a proportion of total costs of goods and services, and this will be well in line with customer's wishes.

Selective employment taxes were also deployed in the late sixties to resuscitate economic life in the regions, particularly in the north and west of the country. The success of these along with a massive increase in subsidies and devolution will lead to substantial rebirth of regional cultural and social life, which in its turn will reverse the migratory trend away from the legacy of nineteenth-century industrial dereliction. Clearing dereliction from the landscape will come firmly within the scope of central government particularly after the Hunt Report on the Grey Areas, and one of the major social contributions of the National Coal Board during its declining years will be to continue its endeavours for the removal of much of the refuse it has thrown up onto our landscape. The NCB did, of course, receive a major fillip from the Aberfan disaster in South Wales. Regional rebirth will have its implications for marketing, which will place yet further emphasis on segmented approaches to customers during the next decade.

A final major element in political and social momentum will be changing attitudes towards credit and savings. The seventies will see the end of savings as a cultural imperative and the widespread acceptance of living on mortgaged future earnings. It is a situation which can be logically rationalized on the basis of confidence in the general economic future of the country and the tendency always present of increasing levels of real income as life proceeds. The extension of life assurance and State pension schemes, as well as the provision of yet more generous redundancy payments and retraining facilities – all these will aid the process. The marketing implications will naturally be manifest in increases in levels of aggregate demand and compounded through accelerator and multiplier effects in the economy.

The general pace of political and social momentum in the seventies can be seen, therefore, to have been conditioned by

36 ORGANIZATIONAL DESIGN FOR MARKETING FUTURES

events in the fifties and sixties. The major unexpected influences will emerge from the transformation of the educational system and the preference in discretionary disbursements for more service, reversing the self-service gallop of the sixties. The violence of individual self-expression will be modified considerably, and this will partially restrain what could in other circumstances have involved a major emphasis on bespoke or custom-built goods. Nonetheless, the trend in this direction will be present and will grow from the increased tendency towards segmented approaches in the sixties reflecting, as they did, the strength of group identification in an increasingly mobile society.

Regional regeneration is likely to be one of the most satisfying economic and cultural phenomena of the decade and commercial interests will not be slow to capitalize on this movement in the same way as they exacerbated the regional problem barely thirty or forty years previously.

A.4. THE CUSTOMER BACKLASH

The majority of customers have, for centuries, been the least powerful factor in the chain of commercial transactions bringing economic goods and services to society. The institutionalization, at a national and international level, of labour was accomplished during the first half of the twentieth century. Employers responded in a similar way; indeed they had no alternative. The contractual immunity which had been built up for trade unions since the Trades Dispute Act early in the century will be finally whittled away in the early seventies. Equally important will be the new attitudes of co-operation in wealth creation which will emerge in the seventies. Exactly a century after the New Unionism had replaced the Chartist mentality in employer–labour relations, what may well be dubbed Responsive Unionism will emerge as a strong factor in British industrial life. It is likely to emerge from two elements in the political situation at the time – firstly the continuing promise from Edward Heath's Government that as and when necessary they will tie the unions more closely into the legal system; secondly, the rude shock which Barbara Castle administered to the Trades Union Congress whilst at the Department of

Employment and Productivity with her proposals for penal legislation against the strike weapon. The strike weapon, in fact, will become a relatively obsolete tool for union bargaining and take on more of the character of frustrated protest, almost of a neo-Luddite variety, where the docks and exports or component manufacturers and sub-assemblers within the motor industry are concerned.

Against this background, customers suffered perhaps most of all, because customers were the last major party to the great commercial debate to become formally institutionalized. Two major roots had, however, been placed below ground in the fifties and sixties in the private membership Consumers' Association and the statutory Consumer Council, even though they both traditionally operated at a point in the process which was often too late to make a major impact. The work, nationally, of the British Standards Institution, and the Weights and Measures Departments of the new, much larger and more powerful civic centres of government, will increasingly be seen to be potentially more effective. A series of scandals in the sixties, in petrol, inflammable nightdresses for children and paraffin heaters, have already given these two organizational foci the opportunity to show their potential.

The laying down of detailed regulations for manufacturers will, in fact, be made easier by the growth of industry co-operation through the Economic Development Committees for a wide range of industries. Customers will no longer need to rely exclusively on the quality control procedures which any manufacturer might or might not care to adopt. In an ever increasing variety of product fields, descriptions will be controlled by law or regulation in the interest of the customer. An important landmark in this direction has been the Trades Descriptions Act of 1967. It and subsequent legislation will prove to be analogous in their effect on customers' well-being to the Factory Acts of a century before, and their emergence was a parallel phenomenon. As had been found in the nineteenth century, without a well staffed inspectorate it was difficult to ensure adequate enforcement. The Weights and Measures Departments of local government will certainly be expanded rapidly to cope with this need.

Private consumer organizations will rapidly recognize that

38   ORGANIZATIONAL DESIGN FOR MARKETING FUTURES

their major role lies not so much in harrying laggard or downright criminal manufacturers, but in making detailed comparisons between one manufacturer's offering and the next in the context of consumer/customer needs. Here the late Consumer Council has already set the lead with the extensive use of the survey method and the publication of product-problems-in-use. The generally less widely based comparisons of products by the Consumers' Association based on 'preconceived' product attributes is likely to be of less value and is markedly reminiscent of a production mentality towards product quality.

As a backdrop to these institutional trends, of course, there will always be the concept of *le client roi*, remaining from the heyday of customer orientation as a corporate philosophy. The legacy in terms of the marketing research function of the business, and systems approaches to marketing management of short-term operations, will ensure that the views of customers, their complaints and plaudits, are all frequently committed to paper, circulated, and used as decision-bases within the organization.

The second facet of the customer backlash will be associated with the movement towards professionalism in purchasing. Although this trend is already and increasingly present in consumer markets, as a result of rising levels of education amongst end-users of consumer goods and increasing educational advertising by the BSI and other interested parties, it will be most clearly perceived in the industrial sector. Once again, a series of national scandals in the procurement of defence aircraft in the sixties has galvanized the government into action. Techniques which Robert McNamara carried from the Ford Motor Company to the US Defense Department under Presidents Kennedy and Johnson – particularly value analysis and cost–benefit analysis – will sweep through the UK government's purchasing activity.

Simultaneously, the aggregation of formerly small purchasing companies will mean massive total buys per annum, running into millions of pounds. To this task will come men of greater knowledge and skills, and the demand for a substantial measure of improved education of subordinates will exist, and will be met by the public and private purchasing professionals, who merged their respective organizations in the middle sixties into

MARKETING'S FUTURE TASKS – SOME SCENARIOS 39

an Institute of Purchasing and Supply with its own pattern of pass degree level professional examinations. The subject will increasingly be taught both on CNAA Bachelor degree courses during the decade, as well as in the technological universities.

The major techniques which will characterize this new professionalism in purchasing are: the rigorous examination of a supplier's ability to supply at the right quality and time, known as vendor appraisal; the rigorous analysis of component parts and technologies to ensure that no shortfall or excess of quality was built into a product or service, known as value analysis; and the careful computation of the benefits likely to accrue from the variety of possible courses of action open to a company and their balancing against the respective costs, known as cost–benefit analysis. This is not all that will be involved, but each of these techniques will represent a qualitative movement away from preoccupation solely with optimum production scheduling and economic order quantities which has dominated so much earlier discussion.

It will lead to increasing domination of manufacturer by the user of his output, and an extension of the concept of custom building in the form of a greatly extended use of detailed product specification. In fragmented manufacturing industries it will lead to the dependence of manufacturers and sub-assemblers on the giant assemblers, such as the Ford and British Leyland motor car companies; or the giant retailers, such as Marks and Spencer, Woolworth, British Home Stores and dry goods chains. This phenomenon has, of course, already been spotted in the massive expansion of Marks and Spencer in the early sixties, based on its own branding and product specification. The basis for this trend is present in almost all sectors.

Countervailing power, a concept enunciated by Galbraith in *The Affluent Society* in the late fifties will prove to be an erroneous diagnosis here. The power of the manufacturer will not be countervailed; it will be removed. Power in the marketing process will remain with one dominant sector alone in most instances. It is just that on some occasions it will be the distributor rather than the producer who wields that power. These several facets of the customer backlash will transform the life of the marketing executive in both the short and longer term. In the short term, customers will have a more immediate contact

40   ORGANIZATIONAL DESIGN FOR MARKETING FUTURES

and a more aggressive concern with the products or supplies they are purchasing. Customer liaison will develop into a much more sophisticated arm of operational marketing in sectors which have hitherto not known it. Customers will also be, on average, substantially larger and the loss of business from such a client will constitute a serious drain on short-term profitability.

Nonetheless, there will be compensating advantages. Wastage through sloppy servicing and quality control will be reduced, and value and cost–benefit analysis will yield improved revenues to customer and producer alike. Although competition will continue as fiercely as ever, the meanest forms of price-cutting will disappear in the face of statutory minima for quality and the like.

In the longer-term planning activities, uncertainty will also be considerably reduced by the partnership which will be built up between customer and producer within the regulations for output imposed by the central government and its agencies. Fewer innovations will turn sour because of a misreading of market and customer needs. Indeed, joint consultative processes between industrial customers and producers will become a vital example for all marketing activity during the seventies. This will be the customer sector where institutionalization will take its firmest hold. The rationale is simply that this appears to be a sector with near equality on both sides of the dialogue in technical expertise and awareness. Such a balance is not so true for the housewife who will accordingly need to be supported in her relatively ignorant state by the continuing involvement of such institutions as the BSI and consumer movements.

A.5. FASHIONS AND FADS

The history of the development of modern management functions is strewn with fashions. New techniques and foci for optimization emerge, accelerate to the status of most important, and decline as rapidly to a sensible and balanced place in the total range of management activity. Production, selling and marketing have all taken their turn during the twentieth century, reflecting as they travelled particular problems that management faced.

The purely fashionable, the exclusively embellishing, phenomena are few. Computers were for a while just such a fashion. Countless organizations took them in at a time when others were doing the same. The purchase of computers attained true epidemic proportions. Acquaintance with this costly disease, just once, was sufficient to bring a careful appreciation to its future purchase. Nonetheless, there was a time in the early sixties when just having a computer in the business was fashionable and gave an appropriate basis for marketing action. In the seventies it may well be the turn of 'design'. The movement for improved industrial design (normally something different from what is currently in vogue is meant here) is already well under way mainly after an initial impetus from the Scandinavians. It has been institutionalized in the Council of Industrial Design which has quickly spread its arms to embrace all forms of engineering design as well. Royal patronage has attached to this sector of industrial activity through annual awards for the 'best' designs. Designers, foremost of whom was probably Terance Conran of Habitat Shops, suggested the Managing Director of the company should be a designer since the product after all, was only different in terms of design from a thousand others. Whilst this particular ideal will seldom be achieved, a wave of aesthetic involvement will surely sweep many companies overtaking not only the products but the packaging, letterheadings and livery of company vehicles.

The distinction between good design and good quality may never be quite clear in most customers' eyes. There is of course, nothing new about functionality of design and its close link with ergonomics. This emphasis, however, will be increasingly important as a basis for competitive advantage. The confusion and the fashion element will focus around theories of the perception of what is beautiful, not only at the visual level but in terms of gratification of the other senses, particularly smell. Perfumed textile fabrics, detergents, packaging materials and the like will be typical of this phase. From it will emerge an important attention to the total process of design in industry and in the distributive trades, and a perceived elevation of aesthetic standards in matters of industry and commerce. Without doubt, however, design will not be a major problem confronting management in the way that marketing, sales or physical distribution were when they emerged in the business.

42 ORGANIZATIONAL DESIGN FOR MARKETING FUTURES

Equally fashionable and faddish will be the pattern of sub-contracting within the traditional marketing sphere of company operations. The phenomenon of university industrial parks and the devolution of research and development activities away from the operational forms of a business will become more and more frequent. The use of advertising agents and marketing research consultants, however, will move in an opposite direction and the relative number of such agencies will fall considerably. Advertising agencies have traditionally served the needs of industrial advertisers poorly. The great bulk of many advertising appropriations for industrial markets have conventionally been expended below-the-line in exhibitions, conferences, display and the like. The nature of the industrial marketing activity has meant that a much greater proportion is spent on personal/technical sales and service than on impersonal, non-technical promotion. This below-the-line pattern will also emerge in those fields more conventionally served by the mass media and may well undermine much of their relative growth. The rebate system between media proprietors and agents will increasingly give way to the fee system of remuneration in the face of this movement.

Marketing research will be taken into the company in many cases where it has previously been sub-contracted, and the entire nature of contract marketing research will change to one of great sophistication, frequently allied with the Business Schools, University departments and Polytechnics. Within companies this will largely be the outcome of the consolidation of efforts by marketing researchers and executives in the context of the systematic treatment of marketing information in totally integrated corporate data systems of planning and control. The intelligent exchange of sales and stock-level information amongst the increasingly large units engaged in manufacture and distribution will also make obsolete many of the former bread-and-butter techniques of the market researcher, such as retail audits and distribution checks. The increasing collusion between media owners and the dominant marketing organizations, particularly in consumer goods, will also lead to a greater but more direct use of experimental facilities for test marketing and mix development.

Since its inception within most companies, public relations

MARKETING'S FUTURE TASKS – SOME SCENARIOS 43

has traditionally been undertaken by consultants working as sub-contractors. The professional PR man has quickly demonstrated his role in the total process, both of internal and external communications. Once the scope for the task is fully realized, it will be but a short step, easily taken in the larger firm, to retract the PR function into the business. Its externalization has always been a somewhat unhappy situation because of the confidential nature of much of the information being handled, and the multiple loyalties of the outside agent.

The transformation of distribution activity on the part of manufacturers has already been alluded to in the context of problem orientation. The fabric of sub-contracting, which during the fifties and sixties normally only embraced transportation fleets, will change. Consultants in total distribution will now offer facilities from the management of on-factory warehousing to ultimate integrated deliveries to end-users or final sorting levels in the distributive process. Manufacturers will begin subcontracting their entire distribution function to agents – not by selling them their stocks but by buying in the managerial skills and the economies of symbiotic distribution at the same time.

An equally fascinating pattern of sub-contracting will emerge briefly in the development of new products through a range of agencies offering ready-made product strategies and development facilities. It will prove to be a transitory phenomenon of the well-known variety where new skills are initially sampled without incurring any permanent or overhead commitment which, when they have proved their worth, are pulled into the main-stream of corporate activity. This has already been the experience of marketing research at large. Peak load-shedding, of course, will continue in terms of commando sales forces and marketing research, but it is unlikely to be a practical proposition in terms of new product development or total distribution.

A sociological cross-current will be apparent in all these movements in the pattern of marketing sub-contract work. The externalization of any activities in the business will reduce the status competition within the framework. It will enhance the co-ordinative role of those who remain internal to the business, and hence their status. Thus, during the seventies the reabsorption of PR and other substantial elements of the promotional activity, along with marketing research, will challenge many of the existing status relationships in the firm. At a total functional level for marketing, however, they will raise the span and content of managerial responsibility, and advance the corporate managerial claims of the incumbents of senior marketing offices substantially. The friction will emerge at the sub-marketing mix elemental levels.

Fashions, fads and fancies are delightfully resistant to prediction. That is their charm and the root of their wickedness. Which fashions and fads will overtake the marketing activity in the seventies beyond design aesthetics and patterns of subcontracting, your Delphic Oracle cannot foretell. Whatever they may be, they will capriciously rob many fine-corporate identities of profits and at times even their very identity. Only the most arrogant manager can tempt fashion by pandering to his own vanity.

PART B

HISTORICAL DEVELOPMENT OF MARKETING ORGANIZATIONS

In Part A we examined a range of scenarios of the future which lies in wait for marketing activities. Here we shall turn our attention to the past in order to identify the evolutionary patterns of thinking about the organizational task in general and marketing's task in particular. We shall do this by presenting an historical perspective on conceptual thinking about organizations and about the disposal of goods and services.

Our review of organizational thought will not take an essentially academic platform since this has been undertaken extensively elsewhere. A thorough treatment can be found, for instance, in J. Kelly's book, *Organizational Behaviour* [Richard Irwin, 1969]; a more popular treatment has recently appeared by Michael Barnes and others from P.A. Management Consultants Limited, entitled *Company Organisation – Theory and Practice* [George Allen & Unwin, 1970]. Derek Pugh, David Hickson and Bob Hinings have also published a most useful glossary of the views of *Writers on Organisations*, which originally appeared [from Hutchinsons] in 1964, but which has recently been revised and is now available as a Penguin book. Here we are especially concerned to demonstrate the strands of thought which have characterized development and the place of the major thinkers in such development.

These ideas constitute the intellectual background against which the organizational *status quo* in British marketing to be described in Part C has emerged.

B.1. THEORY AND PRACTICE IN ORGANIZATION STRUCTURES

The individual working alone does not have problems of

46 ORGANIZATIONAL DESIGN FOR MARKETING FUTURES

organization. He is responsible for his goals and for the solution of problems to achieve these goals, including the decision-making or methods, and scheduling of his activities. As soon as another one or more persons join in working on the task, then an organization is formed. New kinds of decisions are required over and above the technological decisions made by the individual working alone, decisions concerned with the patterns of relationships between those concerned in a joint task. The decisions required of the individual working alone can be summarized as 'what? where? how? and how often?': to these the formation of organization adds 'who?' and 'with whom?'

Pfiffner and Sherwood[1] have argued a convincing case against having any narrow definition of 'organization', and suggest the following as a working definition for the purpose of studying organizations:

> 'Organization is the pattern of ways in which large numbers of people, too many to have face to face contact with all others, and engaged in a complexity of tasks, relate themselves to each other in the conscious, systematic establishment and accomplishment of mutually agreed purposes.'

The important elements included in this definition are numbers involved, complexity of tasks, conscious rationality, and presence of purpose. We need not quibble with Pfiffner and Sherwood's distinction between groups capable of meeting face to face, and larger numbers. Neither should we take issue at this stage with the notion of complexity of task. The division of labour principle is as much concerned with simple as with complex technological processes. Much more important is the notion of conscious rationality. Argyris[2] and Simon[3] have argued that most behaviour in organizations is intended to be rational behaviour; organizations exist to achieve intentions or purposes which are rationally determined. The more vague the perception of the purpose, the less rational the behaviour demonstrated in relation to the purpose.

It should be noted that this working definition allows for a diversity and variety of goals or objectives.

The purposes or objectives mutually agreed by organization members are not the only major determinants of its structure. The shape of the organization will also be determined by the external environment in which it exists, and by its internal environment – the resources available to it.

The mutuality of agreement is itself conditioned by these environmental factors. Mutual agreement does not mean democratic determination of objectives, on Greek city state lines, and may only mean the implied agreement with objectives associated with an employer/employee relationship, but in recent years there has been some movement towards greater 'participation', as part of a wider climate which recognizes the ability and desire of many people to contribute to the most important decisions.

The external environment influences the structures of organizations in a very general sense. This is the macro-environment which includes the economic, social, cultural, technological and legal background. The micro-environment is the market situation in which the organization exists. McDougall and Tookey[4] have suggested that organization structures are affected by various market characteristics such as the number of customers, the state of competition, the status of customers, the stability of demand, the geographical dimensions of markets, the degree of market segmentation, and the unit value of purchases. This analysis is parallel to Woodward's[5] classification of technological elements in the internal environment of an organization. These elements are the characteristics of the methods of production used by the organization. Other aspects of the internal environment which would determine the organization structure would include resources of finance and human skills and any constraints placed upon the use of these resources.

Any formal study of marketing structures must, however, begin with a short resumé of organizational theory built up over the past seventy-five years. It is relevant to modern thinking in the creation of any type of industrial structure and its underlying principles are becoming more important with scientifically designed industrial structures.

Weber's studies on bureaucracy[6] were designed to produce the perfect administrative system – similar to the physicists' concept of a frictionless machine. He established that role is more important than the individual and that no individual should be allowed to create a structure so that his removal would lead to an organization's collapse. Weber's studies were

48 ORGANIZATIONAL DESIGN FOR MARKETING FUTURES

directed at the State, but have since proved themselves elsewhere. For example, Henry Ford's death almost caused the collapse of the Ford Motor Company.

Another great organization theorist worthy of mention is F. W. Taylor[7] whose concept of 'Scientific Management' became so hated that it was banned for thirty years by the U.S. Congress. However, he did establish the earliest ideas of measurement and organization of a task to achieve maximum efficiency.

Arch W. Shaw's[8] contributions to organizational theory are the first directly linked to marketing. He provided a rigorous analysis of channels of distribution and control of such channels exercised by companies. Shaw saw there were different methods of distribution for different types of firm. He used the word 'distribution' instead of 'marketing'. Shaw was followed by a man who might be called the first of the English-speaking practical management scientists, although he did not claim to be so. This was Alfred P. Sloan Jnr,[9] whose plans for General Motors Corporation were introduced after Durant's system of one-man management had broken down and the company was illiquid. Sloan laid down a definite structure of management with tight control at all senior levels. Durant had had up to fifty people reporting to him with the result that he did not really know what was going on. Durant had also emphasized sales volume and not profitability. Such a system might work for an entrepreneur building up a company, but it was non-operable for one of the world's major corporations. Sloan laid down his concept of a company structure in twenty-eight pages of typescript.[10] The final structure may not seem brilliant today but it was workable. He based his plans on two principles:

(i) 'Responsibility attached to the chief executive of each operation shall in no way be limited. Each such organization, headed by its chief executive, shall be complete in every necessary function and enabled to exercise its full initiative and logical development – (decentralization of operation).

(ii) Certain central organization functions are maintained for the logical development and proper co-ordination of the Corporation's activities – (centralized staff services to advise the line on specialized phases of work, and central

HISTORICAL DEVELOPMENT OF MARKETING ORGANIZATIONS 49

measurement of results to check the exercise of delegated responsibility).'

These have now been widely accepted as two principles involved in the construction of any company's structure.

After Alfred P. Sloan Jnr, the concepts of scalar chains and the grand theory of organizations were formally set down by Lydell Urwick[11] in the United Kingdom. He formalized and modified these concepts and put them in the form known today. Urwick accepted, possibly by good luck, the idea of having only a few people reporting to the superior at each level. Urwick's concept of the scalar chain was formalized by V. A. Graicunas[12] in 1933 who maintained that a superior, to be effective, must know and understand his subordinates' relationships with each other. He set the limit at five or six subordinates. Bossard[13] developed Graicunas' study into a Law of Family Interaction – 'with the addition of each person to a family or primary group, the number of persons increases in the simplest arithmetical progression in whole numbers, while the number of personal relationships within the group increases in the order of triangular numbers.'

Since the growth of the theory of scalar chains perhaps the most important addition to organizational theory has been the development of control systems[14] to enable an organization structure to grow. There has also been growing sophistication in the types of control available within the organization divided between wide- and narrow-span models.[15]

A recent addition to organizational theory has come from Young[16] who has suggested that bureaucracy can be replaced by a systems approach incorporating current managerial technologies so that, unlike the bureaucratic system, there will be no constraints. Thus the job of the manager is to design the organizational system – there is no reason why efforts cannot be organized to design a marketing system in the same way that an aircraft is designed.[17]

Sound organization theory is based on principles of specialization, co-ordination and authority. However, these are only the mechanistic elements involved. The earliest scientific thinkers, like Taylor and the Gilbreths, concentrated on the engineering side of the structure and called it 'Scientific Management'.[18]

D

50 ORGANIZATIONAL DESIGN FOR MARKETING FUTURES

The Gilbreths[19] took the concept further and developed time-and-motion study but all of their studies fell into disrepute between the wars because they did not take into account the vital human element. Drucker has pointed out that 'scientific management as traditionally understood assumes that people work best if organised like machines, i.e. linked in series. We know now that this is not correct, for people work well in two ways; either alone, as individuals; or as a team.'[20] This so-called scientific emphasis has, however, been reappearing again and is being applied to marketing in the form of time-and-duty study on salesmen and distributive operations (*Work Study Applied to a Sales Force*).[21,22] The early non-human approach has been steadily supplemented by the work of industrial sociologists led by Mayo and Roethlisberger in the 1930s.[23] Although their studies were not specifically directed at the marketing structure, they had considerable indirect influence and have given rise to many studies of organization charts and the personal characteristics of members of the hierarchy.

Investigations of personal characteristics of members of the hierarchy have shown that the organization chart is only a schematic representation and is often very different to the practical chains of communication on the ground. Waters[24] illustrates this in a sociogram as shown in Figure B.1, which gives the actual channels of communication in an insurance company. Randall[25] also attacks what he calls the *Myth of the Organization Chart*. Analysis of both the expected and the actual channels of communication can yield information which will make the marketing structure more effective, for example by helping with job descriptions.[26] Job descriptions will not stop the growth of informal communication in the structure but will allow a looser, more efficient system which is aimed at solving problems on hand and not just satisfying the 'proper channels'.[27] What we are now chasing is not a superior system but a method of performing a task in the most effective way. This shift towards a middle course of integration, away from exact boundaries as suggested by Weber, and yet not too near the purist human relations school, has been put forward both by Barnard[28] and also by March and Simon.[29] Both have developed systems of organizational theory suggesting considerable integration. They stress the importance from the human

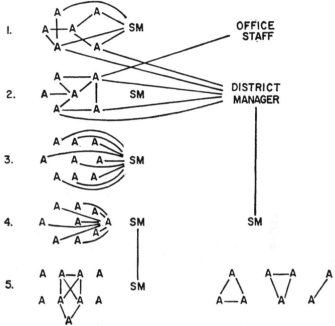

Figure B.1 DISTRICT DYNAMICS (after Waters)

angle of taking a holistic approach rather than looking at the individual's part in the marketing structure. Only comparatively recently has the importance of processual devices for co-ordination, such as committees and venture groups, been recognized and studied in the context of marketing organization structures.[30] One must put this down to the growing sophistication of products and the need to have a wide variety of specialists available to help reach a complex decision.

Marketing orientation and sales orientation have been likened to listening to either the customer or to the producer. There is a strong conflict between the two approaches which often leads to suboptimization. The brunt of the clash is born by the marketing department – this has been well illustrated by Kotler[31] in comparing the conflicting interests of other functions with marketing. Problems of personality again crop up but it is impossible to take them into consideration in the organization chart. For example, a product may be long past the point where it should have been dropped from a range, yet it is maintained

52 ORGANIZATIONAL DESIGN FOR MARKETING FUTURES

because a senior manager made his name with that line, and is determined it will be kept for sentimental reasons. This is often the case with family firms. Such problems are more common with sales-oriented companies because lines are not put through such critical appraisal tests as they are in market-oriented companies.

For a company to decide to change its philosophy can not only be disadvantageous but can create many personnel problems as well. This is all the more important when one remembers personnel have to be trained properly for their tasks and this can often take quite a long time. A different type of problem is found in the firm which slavishly followed a policy of 'promotion from within' because they may find the man promoted into a newly created position has insufficient experience and is without the necessary training.

In a true marketing structure the sales manager is a top-line executive reporting to a comparatively new figure, the marketing director, who is responsible for co-ordinating line and staff functions.[32] The sales manager does not necessarily make a good chief marketing executive because the latter has to think in far wider terms than merely sales and volumes turnover, while the latter has spent his whole working life concentrating on just such an approach. An exhaustive list of reasons exists why the two offices are not necessarily suited to the same person.

Incomplete integration in the marketing structure may occur when the chief executive or some other senior manager exercises his power to prevent the function working properly. The type of character required in a post may vary according to the type and size of the firm. For example, a large firm will need a co-ordinator who thinks in terms of corporate strategy and long-term policy, whilst the medium-sized firm needs a more practical type of person capable of performing some of the marketing task himself.[33] The type of person required must be reflected in the job description. Barrington Associates Inc. have given exhaustive descriptions of the precise characteristics of the marketing director, and theirs has become the classic study on the topic.[34]

B.2. THE EVOLUTION OF MARKETING STRUCTURES

Adam Smith's *Wealth of the Nations*[35] laid down the formal concept of production orientation which remains as the underlying philosophy of many firms even today. The production concept is aimed at maximizing output[36] at a decreasing cost and relies on demand being greater than supply. Thus goods are produced but there is no guarantee they are based on the right criteria. As a result of the production concept the salesman's task is a relatively minor one: he has to sell what the firm has produced. Even in the eighteenth and nineteenth centuries, however, some firms adopted the marketing concept and had a marketing structure of sorts. Boulton[37] relied on prestige buyers and special commissions to spread his name and fame, and gave away numerous sets of buttons to high-ranking officials and well-known members of society. This early era gave us the simplest company task structure of all without a marketing element as such.

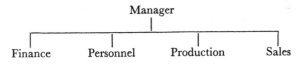

Figure B.2 PRODUCTION-ORIENTED FIRM

Although the structure shown above was the earliest chronologically, it is still widely used. Its main drawback is that there is no feedback of information. One merely makes the product, then sells it. 'Selling focuses on the needs of the seller ... (it) means moving the product'.[38] In other words, the production part of the firm tells sales to 'sell the products and the accountants will worry about the profits'. Most literature currently available merely assumes most industrial organizations have long passed the production state and few writers make more than a passing reference to the sales era. Those writers who do consider sales orientation often look at it as a phase in an evolutionary process rather than as a definite stage in the growth of marketing. Rodger[39] gives a schematic representation of the sales concept in organizational terms, and this is illustrated in Figure B.3.

Lazo and Corbin distinguish between two types of sales manager. They see the new manager as having far wider duties than his predecessors. He used to be responsible for 'the job of day-to-day selling, of hiring and training salesmen to sell;

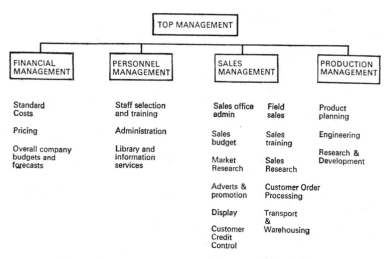

Figure B.3 SALES-ORIENTED STRUCTURE (after Rodger)

order getting was his job, his life, and his responsibility'.[40] They see his new function as being 'responsible for these activities, but in addition, he has the responsibility of transmitting to, and imbuing the men on the selling front with, the new company and management philosophy and thinking.'

The change from either production or sales orientation to marketing orientation is fairly well documented.[41] This wide study has produced analysis at two levels – a general level which merely illustrates the marketing concept in its widest terms, and a second view from other writers which discusses structural aspects of the marketing concept in greater depth, dividing the subject either into functional segments or product divisions.[42] We shall look at these sections in more detail later.

Moore[43] considers the old system of organization laid excessive stress on specialization and centralization while the new marketing structure widens the field of operation. He also maintains that modern marketing organizations are sloppy and slack compared with earlier ones because the organization is now outward rather than inward directed. (This is an issue we discuss at considerable length in Part D, Section D.1.) Reliance is now placed on men and the idea of interchangeability of executives is a dominant factor with the stress on team efforts.

Committees and their fast growing importance have been stressed by Galbraith[44] and many others.

The importance of decentralization[45] in the marketing structure is reflected in committees and in the concept itself – the front man is the one who can discover what the customer wants but this has to be sent back so action can be taken on it. Decentralization has only really become possible with improvements in control.[46]

Moore states that structuring and organization are no longer ends in themselves and that companies today should not attempt to build a single 'best' organization based on a pattern acceptable in every case. Instead, they should seek to produce a logical system aimed at fulfilling the company's objectives and its varied tasks.

Schematic representation is not really possible for the new type of marketing structure but is often attempted. Their authors make too little of the shortcomings and difficulties. These charts cannot take into account communications patterns,[47] characteristics of the individual members,[48] and the relative importance attached to each part of the structure by senior management.

Figure B.4 SCHEMATIC GENERALIZATION OF A TYPICAL MARKETING DEPARTMENT

Recent studies, however, have now shifted from macroanalysis of the marketing system to the much more precise level of operations aimed at solving specific problems. It is this approach to which we must now turn our attention. A fuller picture of the evolution of marketing thinking since earliest times is presented in *Contemporary Marketing*, by Gordon Wills, published by Sir Isaac Pitman in 1971. Chapter 1 of that book incorporates the

56 ORGANIZATIONAL DESIGN FOR MARKETING FUTURES

author's original work on *Caveat Emptor – Caveat Vendor* which looked at the shift in marketing attitudes in the first half of the twentieth century, and his Inaugural Lecture in the University of Bradford, *Marketing Since The Roman Empire*, which traces the thread of marketing activity from Greeks and Romans, through the Dark Ages, the Agrarian and Industrial Revolutions to the dawn of the twentieth century. Interested readers may care to look there for further discussion of this topic.

B.3. STRUCTURAL ALTERNATIVES

We shall now turn to consider the available literature on alternative types of marketing structure currently in use. There is no single 'best' form, but each structure suggested is considered to be the 'best' in a given set of generalized circumstances. We analyse the literature first through a total systems approach and, secondly, through a functional analysis of some of the major subsystems within the marketing area.

The first question to ask is: When should a firm break out its marketing department into separate operations? Literature on this topic is very sparse, and we have only found one study.[49]

The *Journal of Marketing* study gives no data on the exact size and turnover of a department before it should break out but does provide some useful job descriptions. By working back from these it is feasible to discover the size of the organizations before functions were sub-divided.

The study of subsystems within marketing is very recent and in the United Kingdom we have only managed to unearth one of note.[50] Arnfield highlights the role of service in industrial marketing.

There are four generally accepted types of internal marketing structure – functional, product oriented, regionally oriented and customer oriented. Some writers consider a combination of all these types as a fifth variant although we consider it as a natural development.

It is again stressed these structural forms are only generalizations and there is always danger in attempting to emulate an apparently successful organization out of context. Few structures will fit exactly into any pattern because of historical accidents and the personalities of members of the organization. We propose to discuss each organizational pattern in turn and look at its advantages and disadvantages. The functions of the different parts of the organization have resulted from historical developments as well as from the particular characteristics of each firm, the industry, and the class of products it makes. Most functions have a logical allocation within the structure but those which fall in grey areas will be allocated according to the firm's individual characteristics. It is probably because of the difficulty in delineating any really standardized marketing structure that one finds a dearth of literature on this subject, beyond the comparatively short sections which most authors give to the four generalized approaches. Beyond this any data must be empirical although no trace was found of work done in the UK or the USA on organizations in any specific industry. We found some shortage of material on the problems of decentralization in marketing, and the same deficiency occurs with information on delegation of authority in the marketing organization beyond the usual platitudes.

It is generally accepted that it takes several years to introduce and then integrate a proper marketing structure into the firm Allen[51] has argued that any such organization should be built from the bottom upwards at the same time as the upper parts of the hierarchy are altered. The remoulding process naturally depends on the nature of customers and the current abilities of the firm's salesmen. The degree of supervision required is always a problem linked with both the span of control, the individuals involved in the organization, and type of consumer.

Before dealing with the various types of marketing organization we wish to stress the difference between decentralization and divisionalization. The former means passing authority as far down staff and line as possible, while the latter is a result of growth and diversification and may mean one man having total responsibility within the division for its efficient operation.

a. Function-oriented Structure

The functional type of organization is a line and staff structure with the different marketing activities separated into groups, each under a functional head who has line authority. The usual line staff system differs from this because the specialists would have a staff role of being advisers. A typical example is shown in Figure B.5.

Figure B.5 TYPICAL FUNCTIONAL ORGANIZATION

In this diagram there is an arbitrary span of control but it is fairly near the maximum limit. In a somewhat bigger organization one finds the span of control at the top often decreases, as illustrated in Figure B.6. Here a marketing operations manager

Figure B.6 NARROW SPAN OF CONTROL MODEL

and a marketing services manager report to the senior executive, and the functional heads report to these two managers.

This narrow-span model has the advantage over a wide-span model that it allows the chief marketing executive to delegate authority more precisely, thus freeing him to consider long-term

Historical Development of Marketing Organizations 59

and strategic planning problems. The principal disadvantage is the increase in the number of layers in the hierarchy which might distort lines of communication. It is sometimes argued that the narrow-span model creates artificial barriers between market research, advertising and field sales.

The addition of a market planning manager can facilitate close co-ordination in a rapidly changing environment, but overall it can be argued that any marketing structure with a separate sales and planning department without a joint executive to co-ordinate the task indicates a departure from the concept of efficient operations.

An organization is rarely used in an uncombined form by the marketing function and is usually found in conjunction with a line and staff, or territorial, or product type of structure, thus attempting to get the advantages of both systems.

The major theoretical drawback of any functional organization is that people may get orders from more than one individual. For example the salesmen in Figure B.5 receive communications along all the sloping lines, breaking a widely believed basic principle of good organization. This may in turn lead to direct lines of communication being ignored and salesmen dealing straight to staff executives. Finally, there is always present the possibility of conflict between executives in the marketing function, which eventuality can often be dysfunctional.

b. Product-oriented Marketing Organization

There are two main types of product-oriented marketing structure – one based on product divisions and the other on product managers. These can alternatively be viewed as three types of product specialization – product operating specialization, product staff specialization and product functional specialization. We discuss each in turn.

Both approaches analyse the product division model of structure and consider it appropriate for companies manufacturing highly diversified products. In this structure the divisions have very wide discretionary powers and almost full autonomy. They obtain finance and specific marketing services from the centre. The divisions are organized functionally. This is shown in Figure B.7.

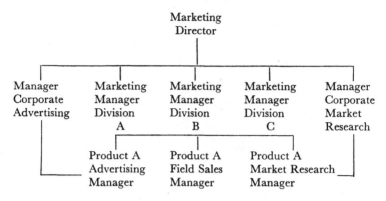

Figure B.7 PRODUCT DIVISION MODEL

The main disadvantage of this type of structure is the old one of dual reporting for product group services. Advertising and market research are both at least partially controlled from a corporate level as well as at divisional level. This can be partly overcome by the mechanics of both services being kept at corporate level in large, specialized departments, and the divisional market research and advertising manager acting as co-ordination or liaison officer. This approach has become quite widespread in the USA in the past few years, at least in market research, and we find the development of the research generalist which is examined in more depth later.

A logical variation on the first product-oriented model is the product manager structure, illustrated in Figure B.8. In this salesmen sell a full range of goods and the product managers

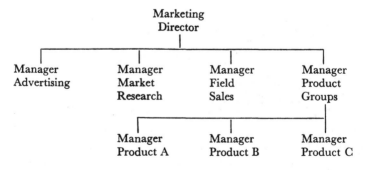

Figure B.8 THE PRODUCT MANAGER MODEL

have no line authority. They can only make recommendations to the line executives. Their advisory role might include planning displays, teaching new uses, and generally helping push their lines from behind. Product managers have recently come very much into favour [52] owing to greater specialization possible in staff departments. This is becoming increasingly important with large-scale advertising budgets and services where one is able to insist that the fullest possible use be made of market research.

This type of structure also offers good training opportunities in general management in the product manager posts. There is high utilization of staff with no overlapping beyond co-ordinating tasks, and these only number one for each product, or group of similar products.

The third type of product-oriented structure is shown by Stanton and Buskirk.[53] This is similar to earlier structures but gives more limited authority to staff members and puts no single person in charge of each product line, as illustrated in Figure B.9. This might appear to provide a saving in staff but probably causes some imbalance in allocation of time between the various products. A structure of this type means only one set of sales staff is required and can sell the full range of goods to all customers.

The principal problem, apart from a lack of co-ordination,

Figure B.9 PRODUCT ASSISTANT STRUCTURE

with this structure is that it does not put a single person in charge of profitability for each line. This can only be overcome by having a marketing manager per product line or group.

Ames[54] has contrasted product managers and marketing managers and derived a number of guide-lines as to which is appropriate in a given situation. If the company manufactures a wide range of products which pass through the same manufacturing or marketing systems, he suggests that the product manager system is best. On the other hand, with homogeneous or related lines appealing to different sectors of a market, the marketing manager concept is preferable as it places emphasis on different opportunities and gives wide authority to marketing managers in their own markets. In each case there are equal numbers of staff without line authority over the full range of activities, so the problems encountered on the human side are very similar.

c. Regionally-oriented Marketing Structure

This structure is utilized by many companies operating over a wide geographical area. Field sales and certain other parts of the overall organization are usually organized on this basis. The exact allocation of other services in the hierarchy varies with their relative importance and regional variations in the

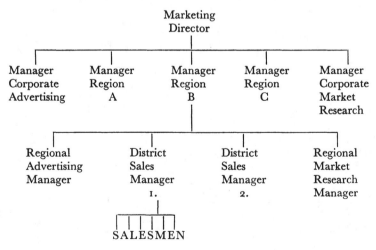

Figure B.10 REGIONALLY-ORIENTED MARKETING STRUCTURE

Historical Development of Marketing Organizations 63

market. In this organization some duties may be duplicated at more than one level causing problems of co-ordination.

A variation on straight regional organization is one where products are sold in two or more dissimilar types of market. We may then find either regional marketing managers for each type of market or national managers dealing with the full range of goods in their type of market. Buell[55] states this type of division is not often found in consumer goods firms although fairly common with industrial goods. It is illustrated in Figure B.10.

A division like this may be the critical element in a marketing organization particularly where the producer is selling a large part of his output to major retail chains. In this case, if single customers are large enough, they may have a special sales manager and even a promotional department allotted to them. The type of person required for such a post is very different from the normal run of sales or marketing manager.

This type of organization is particularly useful for a policy of maximum market penetration.

d. Customer-type Orientation

There are potentially as many different customer-oriented marketing structures as there are customers but we shall only

Figure B.11 STRUCTURE BY CHANNEL OF DISTRIBUTION

consider a few different types. Customer types in large companies often tend to divide by product, thus giving a very convenient division.

Stanton and Buskirk[56] indicate that sales managers in charge of each channel or group are purely line executives responsible to the sales manager, and responsible for a single group of salesmen. They have no staff function. Each salesman in this set-up would deal with a full line of products. In Figure B.11 we illustrate a division by channel and type of business.

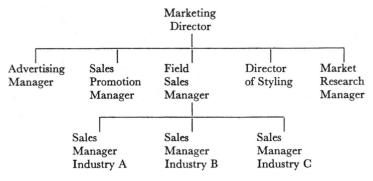

Figure B.12 ALTERNATIVE STRUCTURE BY TYPE OF BUSINESS

The form of organization illustrated in Figure B.12 is gaining ground as specialization increases and as special groups come to be allocated to the 'best' customers or biggest buyers. Specialized uses within an industry would have the same treatment so each industry would have its own group of staff. The organization illustrated may become economically disadvantageous if a major account operates in several industries or utilizes a central purchasing department. There will be opposition to firms who send too many salesmen to call on the same client. The answer could be for specialists to deal with each major account as suggested earlier.

e. Divisionalized Marketing Structures

The largest single problem of a divisionalized organization is the allocation of functions between corporate headquarters and operating units. Buell[57] analyses two principal parts of the problem – the responsibility for profits and costs, and direct functional control. He states that the more that can be passed

HISTORICAL DEVELOPMENT OF MARKETING ORGANIZATIONS 65

down the structure the better. However, there is a proviso: that the divisions must be large enough to keep such services fully occupied and of sufficient size to employ executives of the required calibre. The second group of problems which arises concerns whether management posts should be purely staff posts or whether they should have some line authority as well. Whichever is selected there will be some conflict.

Buell gives a very useful analysis for placing functions in marketing in a multi-divisional company, which is summarized below:

(i) The degree of centralized control depends on the industry and the more decentralization the better.

(ii) Size and cost of the division; big divisions may be sufficient to operate a full range of services of their own.

(iii) Relative experience of divisional managers must be considered.

(iv) Background of divisional managers' experience; if they have wide training they will take the wider responsibility more easily.

(v) Similarity of company products and markets; the greater the similarity the less decentralization required.

(vi) Central placement of advertising may be maintained if higher discounts are obtainable.

(vii) The requirement for a corporate image and definite corporate promotion.

(viii) Type of customer and need for top sales contacts.

(ix) Need for diversification; a company planning diversification will require centralized direction and co-ordination of the search for new products.

Divisionalized marketing structures are described at some length by Buell. One of his first examples is the divisional company with corporate marketing services, a structure commonly found in industrial producers where personal selling is important, for example where there are only a few large buyers.

When the organization becomes sufficiently large it is often found desirable to have some functions carried out at each level – the corporate level has a staff officer and at divisional level the staff are part of line. A structure of this type is advantageous when certain common data may be collected or

E

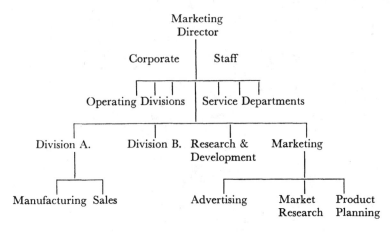

Figure B.13 DIVISIONALIZED COMPANY WITH CORPORATE MARKETING SERVICES

when specialist advice may only be required occasionally. A schematic representation is given in Figure B.13.

Buell suggests centralized manufacturing and decentralized marketing services, a typical organization if the product is to be sold over a wide range of different markets or segments. Geographical divisionalization might also be incorporated in the organization if the firm has to meet a number of locally strong competitors. Such structures were typically once found in the bakery industry and can now be found in soft drinks and con-

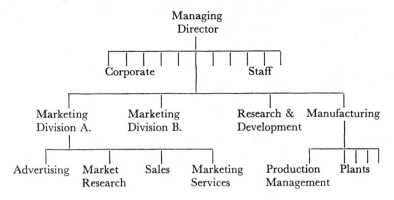

Figure B.14 CENTRALIZED MANUFACTURING: DECENTRALIZED MARKETING

HISTORICAL DEVELOPMENT OF MARKETING ORGANIZATIONS 67

fectionery. A common structure is illustrated in Figure B.14.

The final simple marketing structure on divisional lines is a combination of all these types and may be either fairly simple or very complex. The US National Industrial Conference Board has produced a number of studies of this structure.[58] Mauser[59] gives a full chapter to specific organizations but apart from our own short study on the permeation of the marketing concept in Yorkshire[60] there appears to be very little data available in the United Kingdom.

B.4 THE ORGANIZATION OF MARKETING SUBSYSTEMS

We shall now briefly turn our attention to three constituent systems within the marketing structure – the sales force, marketing research and the new product planning activity.

a. Sales Force Organization

Sales force organization is better documented[61] than most other parts of the marketing structure because it has been under active consideration much longer than any of the other elements. The sales manager is generally deemed to be responsible for hiring, training, supervising and sacking the sales force; he may, in some circumstances be chief marketing executive as well. Sales structures have a special problem caused through the high mobility of salesmen and their widespread distribution over the country. Co-ordination is always a basic requirement and will normally be based on regional sales managers who do most of their communication by telephone. These sales offices are often divorced from the local distribution centres. In the 1960s Proctor and Gamble in the USA divided their sales department into six divisions and thirty-nine sales districts controlling 1,800 soap salesmen, all under a departmental manager for soap.

The problems of structure by areas, products and consumers are difficult to solve in any general formula – the key element is the extent of the differences between products and customers. Thus the division is empirical and often resolves itself through a geographical breakdown at the first level followed by product differentiation at local levels.

The problem becomes far more complex when one considers

68 ORGANIZATIONAL DESIGN FOR MARKETING FUTURES

multi-divisional companies although the same type of analysis can be applied as with a multi-product company.

Aspley and Harkness[62] give a short but practical guide to the creation and operation of sales organizations based on a number of accepted structures. They go into somewhat more detail than any other literature and give a short analysis of staff and line functions. In their analysis of departmental organization they analyse advantages and disadvantages of the various types of organization and lay down a number of 'principles for strengthening the marketing department'.

Aspley and Harkness also posit advantages and disadvantages of centralized organizations. They see the following advantages of centralized control:

(i) Best methods can be imposed on all members of the organization.
(ii) Synchronization of effort; there can be both economies of men and advertising.
(iii) Administration is simplified and somewhat cheaper if centralized.
(iv) Sales territories are more easily manipulated to maintain steady coverage if they can be controlled from the centre.
(v) New plans can be introduced rapidly.
(vi) Centralized recruitment avoids favouritism and nepotism.

On the other hand decentralized control of marketing has a number of advantages:

(i) Decisions can be made by people who know their customers.
(ii) Effective co-operation is obtained in the field between sales manager and salesmen.
(iii) The more authority invested in the sales manager the less will he be treated like a straw boss.
(iv) Field leadership becomes better because the jobs are more attractive.
(v) Organizations can be adapted to suit local conditions and hence be used more effectively.

Thus both approaches have a number of advantages and only when considered in the context of a given situation can one decide which is the best. Every author stresses the importance of the marketing structure being looked at in the longer term to allow for growth of the company and its evolution.

It is possible to organize the marketing department so there is strong centralized control invested in a sales committee based on the regional sales managers and the general sales manager with regular, formalized, meetings and decisions. The regional sales managers can be either resident on territory or at headquarters – there are advantages in both structures.

b. Organization of Marketing Research Departments

Practical evidence on the organization of marketing research appears to be very scarce and we were unable to trace any published studies of UK organizations. In small companies it appeared that any market research is performed in conjunction with other duties or else through the firm belonging to a trade association and obtaining general data from them.

Medium-size companies may employ the above method or may purchase regular data from one of the sub-contract marketing research organizations. Larger companies may employ their own market research departments and also utilize commercially prepared material, especially if the required data can only be obtained from a large number of interviews.

Brown[63] made a study in the USA in the 1950s into market research organizations and this appears to be the only empirical study available. He illustrates a typical marketing research organization, which is shown in Figure B.15.

Market research structures vary greatly not only with the size of firm but with the industry and competitive environment. If

Figure B.15 TYPICAL MARKET RESEARCH ORGANIZATION FOR A FOOD FIRM

70 ORGANIZATIONAL DESIGN FOR MARKETING FUTURES

little or no formal research is done the data collected from the trade association may have to be handed direct to product managers for use at their discretion. The precise functions of market research departments vary widely. In some companies they may be low status groups, while elsewhere they are rated highly. This is often reflected in the person to whom the senior market research executive reports. Individuals in a market research department may not work together but may be attached to individual product groups and report to the product managers direct.

Blankenship and Doyle[64] consider that the total utilization of the market research department will depend at least in part on its physical location within the firm. Organization on a functional basis is illustrated in five different ways – the processing organization is one which only the largest firms can afford and is directed at obtaining meaningful data from raw material at high speed. Applications orientation is a half way setup on the way to a full-scale market research unit, using data from all sources to answer specific *ad hoc* questions. A third possible organization is the brand-oriented structure which is organized so members work on specific brands. The final two structural systems are based firstly on division by technique, which proves very useful for full-size consulting organizations where one department may deal with mass interviews and another with telephone interviews. And secondly, the structure may be built around respondent types – for example one section might deal with housewives and another with purchasing officers.

Marketing research is currently one of the most rapidly growing areas of the marketing activity and has given rise to a new kind of animal, the 'research generalist'. His job is that of liaison officer between the manager requesting a research study and members of the marketing research department. He has to establish mutual trust between both sides and try to see all the problems involved and the type of data required, as well as know what is feasible. He has to suggest plans to both sides and adjust them to fit the objectives and keep both parties happy. A critical element in his job is that of calling in the right experts at the right time and explaining any weaknesses to the marketing manager. In the future much of this task may be filled by the marketing research manager but with large departments he cannot be expected to be fully in touch with all the research in progress.

Whether marketing planning is a legitimate part of marketing research is a matter which is still open to controversy. Often it is within the duties of the marketing research department to look at new products in detail. The AMA have produced a fairly detailed research study[65] on this topic which considers a number of specified companies' planning departments and how they can fit into the firms' overall marketing organization. We shall be particularly concerned with this general issue, however, in Part D.

c. Product Manager or Market Manager?

Within almost any organization of a moderate size, a programme of product innovation will exist and will contain the following specific activities:

   (i) Creative development of ideas
   (ii) Identification of market requirements
   (iii) Technical development
   (iv) Marketing mix developments
   (v) Evaluation of value of project to company

Let us examine these tasks in some detail and consider the organizational implications.

We are specially concerned with the way in which the firm can organize itself to generate more and *better* ideas for new products. Some assistance in managing the creative elements in business can be gained by developing guidelines for recruiting and motivating creative personnel and for constructing an environment which is conducive to creativity. The basic problem lies in the conflict implicit in the organization's need for conformity which is anathema to the creativity of the scientist or technologist. The latter may have joined the firm, not to further its goal, but in order to have better facilities and high salary. Having joined the firm, the highly creative scientist may be less submissive to authority and tradition than other personnel. In particular, he may resent having routine tasks assigned to him. It has been suggested that the best environment for the highly creative scientist is a structure which is less rigid and formal, with the usual traditional controls over operating procedures being relaxed.

72 ORGANIZATIONAL DESIGN FOR MARKETING FUTURES

The question of who supervises the scientist or technologist is difficult to resolve. The scientist will normally prefer a competent scientist. Motivation is a further obstacle. Figure B.16 contains the results of an American survey where scientists were asked to state the motivations behind their creative activity. The reward system operated by the firm in terms of finance, formal status in the organization and special benefits, is shown to be relatively ineffective alongside the principal motivations of a desire to solve problems, personal justification and scientific prestige.

	% Replying
Desire to solve problems	68.6
Personal gratification obtained by accomplishment	64.0
Desire to win scientific prestige	64.0
Desire to advance in financial position	42.0
Desire to advance in title	14.3
Desire to win in competition	12.4
Gaining special benefits (bonuses, trips, vacations, etc.)	4.8

Figure B.16   MOTIVATIONS BEHIND CREATIVITY

One type of reward which is often mentioned – although it may not be in the firm's best interests – is the granting of 'free' time when personnel are able to pursue research hobby horses.

Solutions to the problems of effectively managing the creative function are not easy to find. A possible way of alleviating them is discussed later within the concept of Venture Management.

The identification of market requirements includes the identification of customer needs and thus the generation of ideas for products, as well as a return to the market to seek customers' attitudes towards a partially or fully developed project. In addition to the technical activities of organizing creative sessions, administering concept or product tests, and operating market tests, the interpretation of findings demands a high degree of what we might term creative judgement. Most marketing research does not provide obvious or optimum solutions and it is frequently the task of a marketing executive to employ his subjective judgement. As in the case of scientific and engineering personnel, the management of this activity poses many problems.

HISTORICAL DEVELOPMENT OF MARKETING ORGANIZATIONS 73

Perhaps the most fundamental of these lies in the fact that marketing executives are mainly concerned with the management of existing products. To perform this task well requires skills such as administrative ability, a talent for motivating subordinates and commercial expertise.

The skills required for evaluating and matching product and marketing offerings to a market requirement *in the future* are different and may not be found in the same man. In addition, of course, a manager of current activities may have an adequate work level and tend to postpone activities and decisions on new projects.

New product planning appears to be principally organized in British industry by sharing responsibility between executives from different functional areas who are also likely to have responsibilities for managing present activities. In industries where product life cycles are short and the rate of innovation is rapid, different types of structure have been developed. Thus, we find that it is common for marketing managers of existing products in the pharmaceutical industry to have no involvement in projects leading to new products.

Within the marketing area itself, we may find future organizational difficulties in the way of effective project management. For example, the skills required by a marketing manager are different from those needed by a marketing research executive. The latter will be more analytical, should be more objective, and is likely to be more cautious than the marketing manager, who must balance profit against his desire to see a project succeed, possibly at high cost. An example of how this conflict of attitudes and skills may jeopardize a project is often found in market testing programmes.

Many of the organizational problems that were identified in the management of creativity are equally common in the process of technical development. New problems arise in the transition towards making plans for production, where R & D personnel and production engineers may have to make compromises on the product specifications and the manufacturing process.

Other organizational problems may be encountered when the product and marketing mix have been developed by a full-time new product manager and must then be handed over for continuous operation to a marketing manager of existing products. Any conflicts that arise represent the debit side of making the development of the marketing offering the responsibility of a specialist, a system which also has many advantages.

A series of decisions must, of course, be made at each stage of development on the value to the firm of any project. At the early stages this will involve forecasting the project duration and cost of development. At several stages, estimates of market size, product sales, and profitability will have to be made. These decisions inevitably require subjective evaluation and, in

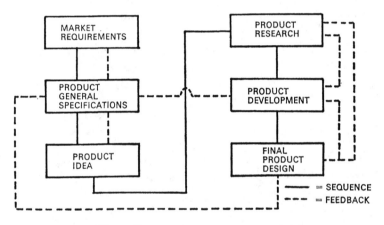

Figure B.17 PRODUCT-PLANNING SYSTEM

the context of the complex modern organization, many people must share in the decision. Estimates of market size and anticipated market share will come from marketing, will be matched with estimates of costs, and be translated by the financial group to expected profit. However, since the subjective element is widely recognized, other personnel – particularly top management – may well wish to revise predictions that have been made.

Clearly, if the project is to go ahead successfully, there is a need for relatively reliable predictions. Also, it is important that co-ordination of the various functional groups in the firm is achieved. Figure B.17 demonstrates some of the necessary patterns of communication. In addition to communication from group to group, each group should have an understanding of the total company goals for the project.

Historical Development of Marketing Organizations

A number of different approaches are in common use, all of which have some disadvantages. Among the considerations that will determine responsibility for the project we can point specifically to the technological content of the product, and the lead time from project initiation to market offering.

Thus, many consumer non-durable goods, in such areas as food, toiletries or confectionery, are the responsibility of a marketing executive during their development stage. This is particularly so when the innovative content is largely concerned with presentation or creating a new image for a specific market segment. There will normally be a certain amount of liaison with other functions: for minor reformulations or packaging developments, financial assessment, etc. If the new product fits very logically into an existing range, this may well be a happy solution. It does, however, suffer the disadvantage that the outlook and attitudes of marketing management may not be sufficiently objective and the task of evaluation may not be performed adequately.

If the technological content is relatively high, the project may be the responsibility of R & D personnel until quite an advanced stage of development. The danger here is that, even in the most market-oriented companies, the subsequent product is well-engineered but not entirely appropriate to market needs. Recent examples of this phenomenon can be seen in the motor industry.

In order to achieve a balance between technological excellence and acceptability to the market, some form of joint responsibility seems to be indicated. The approach outlined by Peterson,[66] of New Venture Management, is now increasingly employed. To review the procedure very briefly, a group composed of personnel from the marketing, finance, manufacturing and research functions is established, forming a company in miniature to manage the venture throughout. Finally, the project may be taken over by another department or even become an operational department on its own. As Peterson points out, a group of this kind can offer the additional facility of a training ground for senior management analogous, perhaps, to the brand management system which is more familiar. The major advantages, however, lie in the creation of an entrepreneurial spirit and in the fact that a group of personnel

76 ORGANIZATIONAL DESIGN FOR MARKETING FUTURES

committed to one objective can possess all the skills to perform the tasks called for in new product management.

Many firms effectively organize their new product management activities by means of a committee, which either has a permanent responsibility for new products or is established on an *ad hoc* basis for a particular project. Members of the committee will be assigned tasks, on the performance of which they report back at the next meeting. A major disadvantage of this system – apart from the definitions inherent in committees – lies in the fact that members are only partially committed to new products.

B.5 SOME EMERGENT PRINCIPLES

Throughout our discussion we have emphasized the importance of company philosophy, policy and objectives which must, in the interest of the firm, its shareholders and employees, be clearly defined before the appropriate type of marketing organization can be identified. We have, in broad terms, tried to look at the sort of analysis managements have been encouraged to make.

We firmly believe that the marketing environment is becoming increasingly competitive for the majority of firms, and that every company lives in a dynamic situation. In an effort to control its destiny more precisely we have suggested that firms should adopt a consumer-oriented approach which can only be achieved through an adequate marketing organization.

We have surveyed much of the relevant literature available on marketing organizations in the UK and North America, finding that a wide range of information is available. Rapid progress has been made since Arch Shaw first wrote on the subject.

From our analysis so far we will now attempt to outline the fundamental principles which seem to be implied in the literature for management when attempting to establish the best marketing structure for its own situation.

Management requires the planning, organization and staffing of a company in the manner most likely to achieve the ultimate objectives of the enterprise, and then the directing,

HISTORICAL DEVELOPMENT OF MARKETING ORGANIZATIONS 77

controlling and co-ordination of the people involved. This means that two factors must be recognized:

(i) An enterprise is a social system with its own attitudes, values and beliefs.
(ii) Because management comprises so many different factors and so many specialists are involved there must be a team effort.

In an efficient firm there is no room for one functional interest to dominate all the others, be it finance, production or marketing. Only by working as a team can all the interests and major factors be taken into account.

If this basic management goal is not pursued, then a wrong decision will probably be made and is likely to be expensive for the company. Thus, when we discuss management organization, we have to work from the most basic concepts.

We have already noted a number of times that a sound marketing organization cannot be created in splendid isolation because of the overriding considerations which must be included:

(i) An adequate corporate philosophy and strategy.
(ii) Sound overall organization structure.
(iii) The right management structure to balance available talent.
(iv) An adequate system of controls.

The duties of top management can similarly be reduced to three basic responsibilities – delineating company philosophy, formulating policy and setting objectives. We examine each of these below.

The foundation-stone for every company's activity is the philosophy or attitude it takes to its activity. If top management considers that its operations should be based on a production philosophy, the functional design of each activity will reflect this. The same happens if marketing or finance is taken as the major segment. Some firms do not attempt to follow any given ideology and may well drift along just surviving with practically no growth and no purpose. It can be argued quite convincingly that contemporary businessmen need a sound marketing philosophy. However, we are concerned with the marketing structure rather than its justification.

78 ORGANIZATIONAL DESIGN FOR MARKETING FUTURES

A confused company philosophy will confuse all the other principles the firm is trying to follow. Top management must have sufficient understanding to be able to lay down these guide-lines, monitor performance, measure final outcome, and review the original philosophy.

Company policy, simply stated, is the mode of thought and body of principles underlying the activity of an enterprise. It will have external and internal aspects. There is also an ethical component involved in policy.

Policy as an aspect of planning involves the following processes:

   (i) Collection and review of facts and circumstances on which policy is based.
  (ii) Interpretation of policy into executive instructions.
 (iii) Proper channels for the communication of policy.
 (iv) Translation of policy into plans and procedures.
  (v) Checking that policy is carried out.
 (vi) A system for review of policy.
(vii) Recognition for review of policy.

There must be some kind of control and rules laid down for subordinates and the distribution of authority. Policy as such is very difficult to show in a company as it is so widespread throughout the firm. Actual policy is not as easy to trace as written policy. A firm is at a great advantage if it can set down a clear policy which is easily communicated.

Based on the premise that a company has a major economic objective – to create customers at a profit – it is important that the company also lays down operating rules as well so it can measure its performance and control its activities. The customer-oriented company must include the following objectives:

   (i) A definite market standing.
  (ii) A conscious policy towards innovation.
 (iii) An emphasis on productivity.
 (iv) Availability of physical and financial resources.
  (v) Planned profitability.

The market standing objective can be subdivided into a number of distinct marketing goals:

Historical Development of Marketing Organizations 79

(i) The standing of existing products expressed in terms of competitive position and in terms of profitability, this analysis further divided into existing and new markets.
(ii) Products and their abandonment considered under a number of headings such as technical reasons, market trends or inadequate profits, and production mix considerations.
(iii) New products needed for given time periods, to increase volume and profit, to complete the market offering.
(iv) New markets required to generate monetary volume and/or as a percentage of the rest of the business.
(v) Distribution channels analysed both for penetration and efficiency for the present and for the future.
(vi) A pricing policy created for existing products and new products.
(vii) Customer service planned under a number of heads specifying the level it must attain as well as a means of its measurement.

We have extracted a number of specific principles relevant to the creation and operation of efficient marketing structures. These principles are comparatively simple but many firms have reportedly encountered serious difficulties when ignoring them.

a. Analysis of Company Needs

The company encounters five main problems in its organization charts:

(i) The division of work at different levels.
(ii) Problems of co-ordination.
(iii) Motivation of employees.
(iv) Problems of a changing technology;
(v) Inadequate communication within the firm.

The principle of division of labour implies patterns of work relations and specialization but becomes less illuminating when considering overall goals. Lateral relationships, as distinct from hierarchical relationships, are very important and are reflected in a number of points to be borne in mind when building a structure, for example:

(i) Work plans.

(ii) Specialist departments.
(iii) Service plans.
(iv) Advertising flows.
(v) Audit flows.

In designing a formal structure it is vital to consider how the informal system will probably work. This is easier if part of the staff has been employed before. The incorporation of the informal system within the formal will enable company objectives to be achieved more easily and will facilitate co-ordination. Traditional planning of organizations has been based on plans such as the following:

(i) Decide on the division of work.
(ii) Decide the basis on which the marketing function is to be structured.
(iii) Determine line and staff relationships.
(iv) Explore how authority will be exercised.
(v) Create organization charts.
(vi) Assess the required degree of decentralization.
(vii) Create job descriptions.
(viii) Consider spans of control.

This is a useful guide but is not broad enough to be wholly effective. A better analysis would also query:

(i) What is the central purpose of the organization?
(ii) At what level will decisions be made?
(iii) How will the marketing functions be related?

With this wider analysis we can include the relevant marketing factors and then, having built up our marketing department, we can fit it into overall management and direction of the business enterprise.

b. Analysis of Human Needs

Every individual is a part of two networks of social relationships – the formal relationships of the organization, and his or her social relationships at work. Work of a routine nature does not always provide personal satisfaction in a job. We must recognize the role of the individual in the marketing organization and consider a number of points, most especially:

Historical Development of Marketing Organizations 81

   (i) Extent of power in the job.
  (ii) Possibility of achievement or creativity.
 (iii) Extent of the skills required.
 (iv) Limitations on status and security.
  (v) Degree of freedom of action.

The aspirations of each individual can be roughly classified as:

   (i) Degree of satisfaction.
  (ii) Recognition of ability.
 (iii) Security.
 (iv) Satisfaction of emotional response.
  (v) Opportunity to vary or expand experience.

The wishes of individuals can be further categorized into five groups:

   (i) Community goals; good job, pay, etc.
  (ii) Economic security; protection from dismissal.
 (iii) Good working conditions; managerial interest.
 (iv) Measure of personal freedom.
  (v) Understanding of the controlling force.

No single goal can adequately explain motivation, and a blend of all these aspirations and more besides must be developed.

c. Structure From The Top

It seems fairly obvious to structure from the top but many executives are expected to produce results without being given the opportunity to select the tools they require for the job. Under such conditions, no manager can really be held responsible for any shortcomings of his subordinates. Thus when creating any marketing organization one must begin at the top and let the senior executive have some responsibility for appointments further down the structure. Our survey of literature has indicated the type of person who should be appointed to the senior position, although the specific person required varies between organizations. A marketing manager in any type of organization must have two basic characteristics:

F

82   ORGANIZATIONAL DESIGN FOR MARKETING FUTURES

(i) He should be a manager in the true sense of the word and not just a specialist, even though he may have come up through the ranks of specialists.

(ii) He should have a sound appreciation of the marketing aspect of business and appreciate the full implications of a sound business philosophy.

Too many companies still have a policy of promoting from within and many inexperienced executives get promoted too early. Other appointments are even made on academic prowess. This is a special problem when one is in a buyer's market. On the other hand, we do not advocate a policy of bringing in an outsider at every opportunity. What we do suggest is a sound staffing policy where the best man for the job is selected regardless of where he comes from, on the basis of careful job analysis.

d. Proper Balance of Talent

Many firms ignore the concept of balancing talent: this includes age, experience, maturity, educational qualifications and sex. For example, the organization should probably not be staffed with people all of the same age-group, so that there is a chance for staff to turn over gradually. There must also be room in the organization for those with and without experience, so that training on the job can be given. Maturity does not only refer to age but also to outlook, hence a marketing organization should include experts from other departments, e.g. a designer or artist should be included in any department dealing with packaging. There must also be room for generalists as well as specialists. Education is also important and there is room for those with marketing as well as with specific technical training in the organization.

Considerable discussion is found of equality of the sexes and problems incurred when women leave, but there are also difficulties encountered when men leave an organization for a better job elsewhere. Many tasks can be carried out just as well by women as by men and there is no reason why they should not be given equal career opportunities to those available for men. In many fields, especially routinized marketing tasks, women will out-perform men nine times out of ten.

HISTORICAL DEVELOPMENT OF MARKETING ORGANIZATIONS 83

e. Staffing with the Right People

There are five major ingredients which should be considered when looking at staffing:

(i) A proper definition of the job.
(ii) Job appraisal and specification.
(iii) Advertising and recruitment procedures.
(iv) Proper induction training.
(v) Adequate staff development.

Efficient staffing requires organizational planning as well as management development. Unless organizational planning is given pride of place, the firm will rapidly suffer setbacks.

Management development has two principal aims in view. It seeks the improvement of skills in present staff, and the provision of executive skills for the future. Such objectives are often best achieved by following a list of seven points of development enumerated below:

(i) Define the present responsibilities and interrelationships in the marketing organization.
(ii) Specify the expected educational, technical and managerial skills required, and also judge the personal qualities and experience needed.
(iii) Forecast future organizational needs and plan for these in the structure.
(iv) Create selection and promotion procedures.
(v) Have specified appraisal of ability and progress.
(vi) Create definite management training.
(vii) Be guided by experience.

f. Design of Adequate Controls

There are three main parts to creating an adequate control system:

(i) Establishing standards of performance in some easily understood form, e.g. hours, cost, units produced. One has to set standards for the present and future.
(ii) Measurement of performance for today and for the future. The more complex the function the more difficult this task.

84 ORGANIZATIONAL DESIGN FOR MARKETING FUTURES

(iii) The company's actual performance must be measurable and corrective action must be taken when deviations occur.

If any of these elements are missing no proper control can exist in the company organization. Control techniques are designed to measure whether actual events conform to plans, and where divergence occurs, to trigger action.

Techniques of control can take a number of different forms but some of the most important are management ratios, budgeting procedures, statistical presentation, management audits and personnel control. Marketing organization control techniques must be concerned with the future so deviations can be corrected as soon as they occur. They must be thought of in terms of people, be capable of being changed if plans change, and must reflect the pattern of organization. Any control system must save more than it costs to be worthwhile.

g. Built-in Co-ordination

The whole purpose of management is to achieve harmony between the various groups and individuals in the firm. People will have different ideas of how company objectives can be best achieved and the firm has to provide some means of linking these different ideas and creating understanding between the different elements.

Constant criticism and rivalry between different parts of the group is a poor co-ordinator, and no instructions 'to co-ordinate' will achieve the ends of the firm. Co-ordination must be built into the marketing structure from the start and cannot be instituted once the departments have become self-contained and insulated from the rest of the organization. The marketing manager must define and explain the dominant goals of the organization to its members so they see where they fit into the overall picture. He can do this best by holding discussions, ensuring information passes in all the required directions, and defining for each management position the relationships involved. There are numerous devices which have been tried to improve co-ordination and co-operation – news letters, house magazines, and so forth.

Co-ordination can only be *achieved* in the marketing organiza-

HISTORICAL DEVELOPMENT OF MARKETING ORGANIZATIONS 85

tion; it cannot be ordered. The best results can usually be achieved by:

(i) A properly designed organization.
(ii) The right selection of subordinates.
(iii) Training and supervision of subordinates.
(iv) Explanation of plans and instructions.
(v) Establishment of proper controls.

Besides having to control and co-ordinate his own section, the chief marketing executive must cope effectively with relationships with other company departments.

h. Evolution not Revolution

Companies are rarely structured initially with a full marketing organization but come to require one over time. The organization should not try to create such a department within the firm too rapidly as such rapid change can be fraught with danger and can turn out to be very costly. The transition from sales to marketing orientation should ideally be gradual to allow people time to adjust and to create channels of communication for the new philosophy and objectives to percolate through the firm. There will also be some need for a little trial and error on the way and a sudden rapid change will prevent this. This is not to counsel complacency, just caution.

Personnel in a sales department will need time to get used to the idea of playing a less important part than the overall department, and all the available evidence indicates that such a shift in emphasis requires time. Far too often management tends to ignore the importance of the human factor in adjusting an organization. A sales department relies very heavily on having the right sort of people in it; they must be carried along with the new structure and converted to the marketing philosophy. Thus adequate communications and gentle change, not a sudden autocratic shift, are two of the most important factors in the creation of an adequate marketing organization.

Thus speaks the literature, the documented conventional wisdom, on marketing organization structures. We shall turn now in Part C to the analysis of how British marketing is currently organized – the *status quo*. We shall see that there is a considerable gap between what the literature suggests is appropriate and what actually goes on.

86 ORGANIZATIONAL DESIGN FOR MARKETING FUTURES

B.6 REFERENCES CITED IN PART B:

1 Pfiffner, J. N. and Sherwood, F. P., *Administrative Organization*, Prentice-Hall, 1960.
2 Argyris, C., *Understanding Organizational Behaviour*, Tavistock Publications, 1960.
3 Simon, H. A., *Administrative Behaviour*, Macmillan, 1957.
4 McDougall, C. and Tookey, D., *Marketing Organization Structure*, 2nd Marketing Theory Seminar, Ashridge Management College, April 1969.
5 Woodward, J., *Industrial Organisation: Theory and Practice*, Oxford University Press, 1965.
6 Weber, Max, *Theory of Social and Economic Organisations*, Free Press, 1964.
7 Taylor, F. W., *Principles of Scientific Management*, Harper Bros, New York, 1915.
8 Shaw, Arch W., *Some Problems in Market Distribution*, Harvard, 1951.
9 Dale, E., 'Contributions to Administration': Alfred P. Sloan, *Administrative Science Quarterly*, 1, 1, pp. 30–62.
10 Dale, E., ibid.
11 Urwick, L., 'Executive Decentralisation with Functional Co-ordination', *Management Review*, December 1935.
12 Graicunas, V. A., 'Relationship in Organisation', *Bulletin of International Management Institute*, March 1933.
13 Bossard, J. H. S., 'The Law of Family Interaction', *American Journal of Sociology*, 1945, p. 292.
14 Goodwin, E. L. S., 'Control: A Brief Excursion of the Meaning of the Word', *Michigan Business Review*, January 1960.
15 Kotler, P., *Marketing Management: Analysis, Planning and Control*, Prentice-Hall, 1967, p. 141.
16 Young, E., 'Organization as a Total System', *California Management Review*, Spring 1968, pp. 21–32.
17 Young, ibid.
18 Taylor, F. W., loc. cit.
19 Gilbreth, F. B., *Primer of Scientific Management*, Van Nostrand, 1912.
20 Drucker, P., *The Practice of Management*, Heinemann, 1955.
21 O'Shaughnessy, J., *Work Study Applied to a Sales Force*, B.I.M., 1965.
22 Maynard, H. B., *Industrial Engineering Handbook*, McGraw-Hill, New York, 1963, Ch. 4, Section 10.
23 Roethlisberger, F. J. and Dickson, W. J., *Management and the Worker*, Harvard University Press, 1939.
24 Waters, C. W., *Applying Modern Management Techniques to Sales Organizations*, Foundation for Research on Human Behaviour, 1963, Ann Arbor.
25 Randall, C. B., 'The Myth of the Organisation Chart', *Duns Review of Modern Industry*, February 1960.
26 Lazo, H. and Corbin, A., *Management in Marketing*, McGraw-Hill, 1961.
27 Kotler, P., *Marketing Management: Analysis, Planning and Control*, Prentice-Hall, 1967, pp. 138–9.
28 Barnard, Chester, I., *The Functions of the Executive*, Harvard University Press, 1938.
29 March, J. G. and Simon, H. A., *Organizations*, Wiley & Son, 1958.
30 Tillman, R., 'Committees on Trial', *Harvard Business Review*, May–June 1960; and Lorsch, J. W., *Product Innovation and Organization*, Macmillan, 1965.
31 Kotler, P., loc. cit., p. 139.
32 Salisbury, J., 'Profile of the Typical Sales Executive', *Sales Management*, 19 February 1960, p. 33.
33 Felton, A. P., 'Making the Marketing Concept Work', *Harvard Business Review*, July–August 1959, p. 59.

Historical Development of Marketing Organizations 87

[34] Barrington Associates Inc., *The Kind of Executive Needed for the Position of Vice President Marketing*, Barrington Associates, New York, 1957.

[35] Smith, Adam, *The Wealth of Nations*, Methuen, 1776; Dent, 1910.

[36] Keith, R. J., 'The Marketing Revolution', *Journal of Marketing*, 1960, pp. 35–8.

[37] Robinson, E., 'Eighteenth Century Commerce and Fashion: Mathew Boulton's Marketing Techniques, *Economic History Review*, 1963, pp. 39–60.

[38] Koch, E. G., 'New Organization Patterns for Marketing', *Management Review*, February 1962, p. 4.

[39] Rodger, L. W., *Marketing in a Competitive Economy*, Hutchinson, 1965.

[40] Lazo and Corbin, loc. cit., p. 231.

[41] Keith, R. J., loc. cit., p. 36.

[42] Bund, H. and Carroll, J. W., 'Changing Role of the Marketing Function', *Journal of Marketing*, 1957, pp. 298–325.

[43] Moore, D. G., in Lazer & Kelly, *Managerial Marketing: Perspectives and Viewpoints*, Irwin, 1963, pp. 24–8.

[44] Galbraith, J. K., *The New Industrial State*, Hamish Hamilton, 1967.

[45] Lawrence, P. R., *Changing of Organizational Behaviour Patterns*, Harvard University Press, 1958.

[46] Goodwin, E. L. S., 'Control, a Brief Excursion into the Meaning of the Word', *Michigan Business Review*, January 1960, pp. 13–17.

[47] Anderson, R. G., 'Patterns of Communication in Marketing Organization', *Journal of Marketing*, 29 July 1965, pp. 30–4.

[48] Mauser, F. F., *Modern Marketing Management*, McGraw-Hill, 1961, p. 298.

[49] Bund, H. and Carroll, J. W., 'Changing Role of the Marketing Function', *Journal of Marketing*, January 1957, pp. 273–86.

[50] Arnfield, R., 'The Role of Service in Industrial Marketing', *British Journal of Marketing*, 2, 1, pp. 24–36.

[51] Allen, Louis A., *Management and Organization*, McGraw-Hill, 1958, pp. 73–4.

[52] Printers' Ink, 'Why Modern Marketing Needs the Product Manager', *Printers' Ink*, 14 October 1960, pp. 25–30.

[53] Stanton, W. J. and Buskirk, R. H., *Management of the Sales Force*, Irwin, 1964, pp. 113–14.

[54] Ames, B. C., 'Product Manager or Market Manager?', *Harvard Business Review*, November–December 1963, pp. 141–52.

[55] Buell, V. P., *Marketing Management in Action*, McGraw-Hill, 1966, pp. 80–1.

[56] Stanton and Buskirk, loc. cit., pp. 118–19.

[57] Buell, V. P., loc. cit., pp. 83–91.

[58] National Industrial Conference Board, 'Charting the Company Structure', *Studies in Personnel Policy*, 1959.

[59] Mauser, F. F., loc. cit., Ch. 12, pp. 306–30.

[60] Baker, M., Braam, T. and Kemp, A., *The Permeation of the Marketing Concept in Yorkshire Industry*, Management Centre, Bradford, 1967.

[61] Aspley, J. C. and Harkness, J. C., *Sales Manager's Handbook*, Dartnell, 1962, 9th edn, Section 33, pp. 311–20.

[62] Aspley and Harkness, loc. cit., pp. 40–5 and 311–20.

[63] Brown, L. O., *Marketing and Distribution Research*, Ronald Press, 1955, pp. 30–35.

[64] Blankenship, A. B. and Doyle, J. B., *Marketing Research Management*, American Management Association, 1965, pp. 42–61.

[65] Miller, E. C., *Marketing Planning: Approaches of Selected Companies*, American Management Association, Study 81, 1967.

[66] Peterson, R. N., New Venture Management in a Large Company, *Harvard Business Review*, 45, May/June, 1967.

PART C

BRITISH MARKETING
ORGANIZATIONAL STATUS QUO

C.1. INTRODUCTION

Hitherto, we have looked ahead to the patterns of marketing organization which may well emerge in the future, and we have considered the tradition of research which has examined the scope of marketing tasks and delineated the patterns of marketing organization structures developed to perform these tasks. In this part of the book, we introduce findings from a major new programme of research which has examined the diversity of marketing tasks incumbent on present-day business organizations in the UK and has sought to throw light on the patterns of organization. Although previous studies have examined current structures in depth, this approach has limited them to considering a small number of organizations. The present study has adopted a quite different approach, in that we have received information from a great number of our largest and most important companies. The advantages of this approach are that we have been able to throw light on a much more representative cross-section of contemporary business practice and, in addition, to highlight the principal differences between companies of different size and between the very broad sectors of industrial activity. Clearly, this approach has the disadvantage of not showing in depth the behavioural mechanisms which form the relationship between task and structure, so well delineated in the micro-cosmic studies of, for example, McDougall and Tookey.*

This is a particularly appropriate point in time at which to study the actual pattern of organizational structures for marketing in British industry. In recent years, marketing has become a

* McDougall, C. and Tookey, D., 2nd Marketing Theory Seminar, Ashridge Management College, April 1969.

89

90 ORGANIZATIONAL DESIGN FOR MARKETING FUTURES

fashionable business philosophy as a result of several new developments. The increasing competitiveness of the commercial environment has made it necessary for the individual enterprise to exploit to the full the techniques and procedures which can lead to a better understanding of market demand and greater efficiency in meeting these requirements. As we might expect, a great deal has been learnt from experience in the United States and we have borrowed many marketing techniques, including the common patterns of organizing our marketing activities. At the same time, we have recently seen rapid changes in the affluence and discretionary spending power of the population. Our ability to understand these changes and profit by them has led to the development of a marketing research industry which, by virtue of its technical sophistication, has acquired an international reputation. Of the other factors which have produced our present concern with marketing, we should remember the roles of the professional organizations and the spectacular growth in management education which has occurred during the past decade.

In the now well-established way in which the British have shown a capacity for self-denigration, many pundits have pointed to the depressingly negative reaction of industry to the marketing concept and its operational implications. We have been accused of being rooted in the ages of product orientation and sales orientation and of allowing our more progressive competitors abroad to steal an advantage. Certainly there is some evidence that managers in some industries have shown uneasiness and, on occasions, reluctance to accept the implications of the marketing concept. The present study has, however, served to demonstrate that the senior managers in a great many of our most important companies have an adequate awareness of the operational needs of the marketing concept and have shaped their activities into patterns which to a certain extent reflect the diversity and sophistication of the pattern of tasks required when accepting this concept.

Whilst this is, in a global sense, extremely encouraging, we must introduce the necessary qualifications. Our study is concerned with the patterns of activity which are found in companies which have an annual turnover of at least three-quarters of a million pounds per annum. Thus, we have excluded from our investigation the multitude of companies whose turnover is less than this figure. In addition, we have found that sophistication in terms of acceptance of the marketing concept and willingness to apply it in operational terms is related strongly to size of company – whether this be measured in terms of turnover or number of employees – and to the principal nature of business activity. Thus, the report of contemporary business practice (which follows) will take pains to emphasize the differences to be found in companies having different characteristics.

A note on the methodology employed in this study is called for at this point. The universe which was sampled consisted of all business enterprises in the United Kingdom whose annual turnover was in excess of three-quarters of a million pounds. A list of such companies obtained in 1968 from the then Board of Trade provided a total of 2,400 firms. It was decided that all firms in this list should be contacted and a small proportion was asked to provide information in a personal interview situation which yielded substantial qualitative and illustrative material. This qualitative information enabled us to construct a postal questionnaire which was distributed to the remaining firms on the register. Allowing for firms which were not appropriate to our inquiry for a number of reasons, such as liquidation or the inappropriate nature of business activity, we obtained replies from well over half of all companies in this size category. Fully completed questionnaire forms were returned from a total of 553 firms.

The principal focus for our questioning was the chief executive who, we believe, is in the best position to report and explain his firm's marketing activities and structures within the context of his firm's total operations. Most of our information does, in fact, come from this source, with the major rider that for some detailed information on, for example, patterns of promotional activity, the chief executive consulted his chief marketing executive. This title is somewhat arbitrary and may result in a measure of confusion. In effect, all it means is that executive within the firm who is primarily responsible for the execution of those tasks which are commonly regarded as marketing activities. As we shall see in our report on the findings, such individuals may have a variety of titular designations and, more important, a diversity of functional responsibilities.

C.2. THE CHIEF MARKETING EXECUTIVE

As indicated in our introduction, the executive who is responsible for the performance of marketing tasks may be designated in a variety of ways. Whatever his actual designation, we have chosen to refer to this individual, here and subsequently, as the 'chief marketing executive'. Traditionally, where a company has seen its business philosophy primarily as a matter of distributing its output to a network of customers, we should expect to find an emphasis on sales in the responsibilities and formal designation of the executive responsible for interfaces with the market. In fact, this phenomenon is remarkably long lived and contrasts with other findings in our study which indicate a high level of verbal acceptance of the marketing concept and patterns of functional responsibilities which transcend the narrow task of achieving target ex-factory sales levels. In fact, the single most common title found is that of sales director (in 30 per cent of all companies), followed by that of marketing director (25 per cent) and managing director (14 per cent) (Table C.1).

TABLE C.1 *Title of Chief Marketing Executive*

N = 553	Total %
Sales Director	30
Marketing Director	25
Managing Director	14
Marketing Manager	9
Sales Manager	8
Commercial Director	2
Others	12
	100

More than two-thirds of all chief marketing executives hold appointments at the level of director. This includes an important minority of chief executives who are personally responsible for the performance of marketing functions. The interesting features of the occurrence of the titles of sales director and managing director are largely explained by the size of firm. It is only to be expected that, in relatively small companies directors and other executives will have wide responsibility; in fact in the present study it was much more common to find the managing director responsible for marketing functions in the smallest size categories. Nevertheless, we are only dealing here with companies whose turnover is reasonably large, namely, in excess of three-quarters of a million pounds per annum. It is no surprise, therefore, to find that the same trend is much more common in certain industries, such as construction, whose patterns of managerial activity have traditionally been less sophisticated than in, say, consumer goods industries. The title of marketing director was more frequent in companies within the largest turnover groups and in those firms whose principal business activity is the manufacture of consumer goods. These firms have not only implemented the marketing concept in terms of the title of the executive responsible for marketing tasks; as we shall see later they have also allocated more extensive responsibilities to him.

It should of course be remembered that formal titles do not necessarily indicate differences in the nature and sophistication of the tasks performed by chief marketing executives. Indeed, it is evident that, in the case of managing directors, many may well be performing relatively simple marketing tasks in comparison to those of a marketing manager in a large and sophisticated company.

A measure of the importance accorded by the firm to the marketing function has frequently been seen in the relative status accorded to the chief marketing executive *vis-à-vis* the chief production executive. Our study revealed that in the majority of companies both executives have the same formal status. Where a formal status differential does exist it is likely to be in favour of the marketing executive, who in a quarter of companies ranked higher than his counterpart in the production area, compared to one in ten firms where the production executive has higher formal status.

Elsewhere, we have referred to the rapid development in recent years of management education. By virtue of the uncertainty and frequently unmerited mystique which has attached to the marketing function, substantial resources have been allocated to programmes of training and education in the marketing area. In the firms which we examined, almost three-quarters of chief marketing executives had attended at least one formal course in marketing. Although the content of these

94 ORGANIZATIONAL DESIGN FOR MARKETING FUTURES

courses may range from the introductory or appreciation type to the highly technical, such educational programmes may well have made an important contribution to the firm's orientation and account substantially for the unexpectedly high degree of expressed market orientation which was found in our research.

a. Responsibilities of the Chief Marketing Executive

Table C.2 contains the broad findings of our research regarding the tasks of the chief marketing executive. For some of these, he may be solely responsible; for others he may share responsibility with executives from other functional areas. In some instances, he may have no responsibility for a task which is either

TABLE C.2 *Functional Responsibilities of Chief Marketing Executive*

Function		Responsibility			Not Applic-able	No Re-sponse	Total
		Full	Shared	Nil			
N = 553							
Sales Forecasting	%	56	39	2	1	2	100
Marketing Research	%	56	31	1	6	6	100
Advertising & Promotion	%	58	34	2	2	4	100
Overseas Marketing	%	33	32	10	15	10	100
Pricing	%	34	57	5	1	3	100
Physical Distribution	%	19	34	30	8	9	100
Packaging	%	21	35	18	18	8	100
Public Relations	%	34	45	8	7	6	100
Marketing Staff Selection and Training	%	53	36	2	4	5	100
New Product Planning	%	20	65	3	6	6	100

historically thought to be a part of a marketing executive's total role or which, like physical distribution, is increasingly coming to be seen as a logical part of the firm's total offering to its market. With the exception of the achievement of sales targets, this table provides a virtually comprehensive view of the functional tasks of marketing activities in contemporary business. Let us look first of all at each specific task in turn. As far as sales forecasting is concerned, over half of all chief marketing executives enjoy sole responsibility for performing this function. In an important minority of firms, responsibility is shared and we can easily see here the need for liaison with, for example, production managers and stock control executives. It appears that the corporate contexts under which full responsibility is more likely to be given to the chief marketing executive include being manufacturers of consumer goods, and all firms which have a relatively high turnover.

Although we shall return again to the questions of responsibility for marketing research and the patterns of organization which have been developed to perform this broadly-described task, it is important to note that in the great majority of cases the chief marketing executive exercises at least partial, and in most cases full, control over this important activity. Once again, larger companies, particularly manufacturers, are more likely to accord him full responsibility. Our investigation did not seek to establish which executives within the firm might share in this responsibility and we can therefore only hazard educated guesses. The authors have, for example, encountered a number of cases where the chief marketing executive has played an important part in commissioning *ad hoc* marketing research studies, especially where the chief marketing executive has emerged from a background of responsibility for sales and continues to perceive this as his major task.

Responsibility for advertising and promotion is even more clearly in the court of the chief marketing executive. Nevertheless, an important minority, one-third, have to share their responsibility with other executives in the firm. In the case of overseas marketing, the relatively high proportion of firms in the larger size groups who accorded no responsibility to the chief marketing executive demonstrates that, as size increases, export marketing is commonly established as a discrete and specialist task.

The way in which responsibility for the determination of prices is allocated has often been taken as an indicator of the degree of market orientation within the firm. Historically, prices were commonly determined on the basis of 'cost-plus' and represented the outcome of severely mathematical calculations carried out by accountants. More recently, marketing theorists and practitioners have advocated the adoption of a market-oriented approach to pricing which has regarded the demand function as being composed of behavioural as well as mechanistic elements. Although we shall return to this question later when considering the basis for pricing policies, the allocation of responsibility for this task in itself indicates the shift in

96 ORGANIZATIONAL DESIGN FOR MARKETING FUTURES

orientation. In one-third of companies, the chief marketing executive has sole responsibility for pricing and in almost all other companies he shares his responsibility. Only slight differences are found in companies within the various size categories, with a slight tendency for larger firms to give sole responsibility more commonly. Interesting variations occur amongst different industries; for example, firms in chemical and electrical engineering manufacture are much more likely to give full responsibility to the chief marketing executive, whereas industrial groups whose reluctance to follow this trend is most marked include timber, furniture and paper, printing and publishing.

Physical distribution has traditionally been regarded as a strongly mechanistic activity which could be safely entrusted to relatively junior management. Recently, marketing management has focused great attention on this function as an important element in its overall programme of meeting customer needs effectively, specifically by optimizing levels of service in relation to costs. As a result, physical distribution has come to be regarded as an increasingly important element in the marketing mix. To a certain extent, our findings reflect this trend, in that over half of all chief marketing executives are at least partially involved; however, only one in five exercises complete control over this function. Firms in the largest size category show a marked tendency to be in the van of that trend towards giving the chief marketing executive full responsibility, but the smallest firms also ascribe a higher than average level of responsibility to their chief marketing executive.

Packaging is another task which has traditionally been largely performed by executives outside the marketing area. Considerations of cost, strength and durability have carried more weight than the display and communication roles of packages; thus it is no great surprise to find that only one in five companies grant full responsibility to the chief marketing executive, with a further third where the chief marketing executive is partially involved in decision-making in this area. Differences are marked between firms of different business activity, with the large manufacturers of consumer goods frequently allocating sole responsibility to their chief marketing executive.

Public relations is a further function for which the chief

marketing executive is solely responsible in only a minority of firms, yet is partially involved in most other companies. Manufacturers of consumer goods show an above-average inclination to give sole control to the chief marketing executive. In the case of marketing staff selection and training, we found a much greater concentration of responsibility with the chief marketing executive.

New product planning is a task which has always posed great organizational problems. In Part B we indicated some of the varied approaches which have been adopted in the past, ranging from sole control by a marketing executive or by R & D personnel to some form of group management by, for example, committee, or, more recently, venture groups. The patterns which we have found in the present study hint at this diversity and at the multi-disciplinary nature of the fundamental creative, evaluative and control tasks to be performed. Thus, only one in five chief marketing executives enjoys sole responsibility for the planning of new products but as many as 85 per cent of all firms involve him at least partially. Larger companies and manufacturers of consumer goods accord him full responsibility much more frequently than is the case with manufacturers of industrial goods.

Having examined the responsibility status for the performance of the major marketing tasks, it is salutary to examine the consequent patterns of functional responsibility which are accorded to the individual designated as responsible for marketing. Our analysis led us to identify distinct patterns of functional responsibility and they allow us to come to useful conclusions on the patterns of responsibility allocation to be found in our largest firms.

The first group of firms comprises those where the chief marketing executive is fully responsible for all or most marketing functions. Only 23 per cent, or one in four, of all firms conform to this pattern. This is in substantial conflict with the dictum that the concept of the chief marketing executive requires that responsibility for the *integration* of and *interaction* between the several elements of the marketing mix should be exercised by one man. In effect, we have found that responsibility for the major functions which are commonly regarded as marketing tasks is substantially diluted amongst a number of senior

G

98   ORGANIZATIONAL DESIGN FOR MARKETING FUTURES

executives. The implications are serious. In leading firms in British industry, we have advanced in only a half-hearted fashion to the full operational implementation of the marketing concept in spite of other findings which, as we shall see later, show that a high level of awareness of the marketing concept is to be found, and attitudes are expressed which indicate verbal acceptance of the concept's implications. By far the most common pattern of functional responsibility allocation – found in three-quarters of all firms – is that wherein the chief marketing executive is fully responsible for but a small number of so-called marketing tasks, but shares responsibility for all or most of the others. Few or the firms investigated conform to any different pattern. The very common incidence of firms displaying the second pattern highlights the present situation in which we allow the chief marketing executive to be widely *involved,* but fail to give him that due *control* that is logically inherent in the marketing concept.

C.3.   THE MARKETING DEPARTMENT

Thus far, we have focused our attention in this *status quo* report, on empirical evidence concerning the senior individual who is given responsibility for marketing activities within the firm. It is appropriate now to look at other aspects of the marketing organization structures which we have found and to place them in the context of our knowledge of organizational phenomena. It is here that we are made most aware of the disadvantages of attempting to draw data from a representative sample of companies. Ideally, we should like to examine not merely the external props of organization, such as the usage of committees and organization charts, but we should like to study the actual behaviour of organizations over time. Thus we are not able here to look beneath the surface of task specialization, delegation, authority, co-ordination and control. We concern ourselves therefore with looking at the institutions and the presence of certain major patterns of organization and behaviour.

If we consider first of all the size of the department to which the chief marketing executive must delegate his own responsibilities, most commonly firms have less than ten people

BRITISH MARKETING ORGANIZATIONAL STATUS QUO 99

employed in total in the marketing area. Overall, a majority of firms have less than thirty people working in the marketing field. At the other end of the scale, 14 per cent of all firms have between 100 and 400 personnel in the marketing area; thus, a great variety is to be found in the size of marketing group.

The size of the marketing group is related strongly to the size of firm, but no strong relationship exists between the size of the marketing group and the principal nature of business activity. At this point, we must attempt to introduce definitions of marketing personnel. Clearly, these can encompass highly qualified and responsible executives together with salesmen and clerical staff. Thus, when we look beyond this global structure, we will find that very few firms have more than ten full-time executives employed in the marketing area and that it is most common, even in firms within this turnover category, to find that sales forces have less than ten members (Table C.3).

TABLE C.3 *Number of Personnel in Marketing Area*

N = 553	All personnel in marketing	Full-time executives	Members of sales force
	%*	%*	%*
Below 10	25	72	46
10–19	18	9	15
20–29	10	4	8
30–39	7	2	5
40–49	3	—	4
50–59	4	1	2
60–69	2	1	2
70–79	2	1	1
80–89	2	—	—
90–99	2	1	2
100–399	14	—	6
400–599	1	—	1
600 and over	3	—	—

* *Here, and elsewhere in Part C, where % columns do not sum to 100 it is due to uncertainty or inability of respondent companies. All % calculations are based on the full sample taken.*

As might be expected, the number of full-time marketing executives increases with company size. Once again, there exists a positive relationship between total company size and the number of salesmen, although, overall, four out of five companies have less than twenty salesmen.

Subordinate to the chief marketing executive we are likely

100 ORGANIZATIONAL DESIGN FOR MARKETING FUTURES

to find a great diversity of executives who are responsible for performing the tasks which must necessarily be delegated. Table C.4 reflects the diversity which was in fact found in our study.

TABLE C.4 *Titles of Personnel Reporting to Chief Marketing Executive*

N = 553

	%
Sales Manager/General Sales Manager	50
Advertising Manager/Commercial Manager	15
Export Managers	15
Marketing Manager/Marketing Director	14
Field Sales Manager	13
Salesmen	12
Sales Administration Managers	12
Product/Brand Manager	10
Customer Service Manager/Technical Service Manager	8
Public Relations Managers	7
Distribution Managers	5
Sales Promotion/Merchandising Manager	5
Market Research Personnel	5

In spite of the fact that the most common group of chief marketing executives consisted of sales directors or sales managers, the subordinates of the chief marketing executive were most commonly managers of the sales force. As many as 50 per cent were sales managers/general sales managers and this group far outweighed other groups of subordinates who had quite different responsibilities. These included advertising managers – whose responsibilities are normally concerned with managing the total impersonal promotion efforts of the firm and, at least in so far as formal designation is concerned, represent a carry-over from the past – together with export managers, who are equally common. Since marketing directors and marketing managers are found to occur in at least 14 per cent of companies in a position subordinate to the chief marketing executive, it must be assumed that in a sizeable minority of firms an important marketing executive is made responsible to another executive who may well have broader marketing responsibilities. It is worthwhile to note the position of market research personnel, who are only found reporting to the chief marketing executive in one in twenty companies.

Almost every title of subordinates reporting to the chief

marketing executive was more commonly found in larger companies, reflecting the greater specialization required. The only important exception was in the case of sales administration managers, who were relatively most common in those companies whose turnover was below £10 million and almost non-existent in companies of larger size. We might also remark on the relatively low incidence of product managers and brand managers (or assistants), particularly in view of the research tradition which points to the appositeness of such appointments. As we might expect, product managers are more commonly found amongst manufacturers of consumer goods.

The existence of written-down organization charts is strongly related to the size of company. Overall, organization charts are used by 69 per cent of all firms, whereas in the largest size category the proportion rises to 95 per cent. Where charts exist, their content varies according to the diversity of marketing tasks to be performed and the relative sophistication of the company's orientation.

Further, the presence of organization charts is strongly correlated with the use of written-down job specifications for marketing executives and indeed for all company executives. The use of organization charts may, as we have seen, reflect a number of organizational symptoms. They may be regarded as ideals which the actual communication system may follow only very little, or they may portray the real patterns of formal and informal communication and responsibility which are to be found in the company. If we adopt the latter, more generous, viewpoint the extent to which organization charts are to be found indicates a high level of concern with delineating the behaviour patterns of the organization. In the same way, we can interpret the wide presence of job specifications, found in 57 per cent of all firms, as indicative of the preoccupation of most firms with formally portraying the division of the organization's tasks between its various executives.

In companies with small or medium-sized turnover it is often possible for the chief marketing executive to supervise all marketing activities within the firm. On the other hand, large enterprises often find it necessary to divide their marketing activities according to a number of relevant criteria. These may be the product groups of the company, the geographical

102   ORGANIZATIONAL DESIGN FOR MARKETING FUTURES

areas in which it operates, its different types of customers or, indeed, a combination of these criteria. The most common way of dividing the marketing tasks is according to product groups (59 per cent of companies) followed by geographical area (44 per cent) and customer (32 per cent). Frequently, companies use a combination of these to divide their marketing activities, particularly those companies in the largest size groups. A breakdown of activities along geographic lines is most commonly found in smaller firms, whereas manufacturers of consumer goods are more likely to divide their marketing tasks according to product range.

C.4. EXTERNAL AGENCIES

Even in the very largest companies, it is more effective and frequently more economical, to delegate responsibility for performing certain tasks to outside agencies. Table C.5 contains the findings from our study on the extent to which some important tasks are sub-contracted in this way.

TABLE C.5 *Use of External Agencies*

| | External agencies | | | |
N = 553	Used partly/ occasionally	Used entirely	Not used	Not appropriate
	%	%	%	%
Display/Pack Design	39	10	19	21
Advertising	45	39	9	4
Marketing Research	47	7	31	7
Public Relations	35	14	35	8
Transport of Finished Goods	46	13	25	10
Sales Operations	19	—	59	9
Customer Credit/H.P.	25	5	43	20

External agencies are most commonly used for advertising; this is to be expected in view of the specialization required to perform this task. Marketing research and transport of finished goods were also at least partly or occasionally sub-contracted in over half of all companies and, at the other end of the scale, sales operations and customer credit/H.P. are normally managed within the company's own resources.

The extent to which a function is delegated externally is

BRITISH MARKETING ORGANIZATIONAL STATUS QUO 103

very closely related to the nature of the company's business. Thus, consumer goods manufacturers, who have generally speaking a much greater and more consistent need for developing display and packaging, make much greater use of outsiders, with a total of 77 per cent doing so at least partly or occasionally. The same basic pattern is found for advertising and marketing research. The reverse applies, however, in the case of customer credit/H.P., where manufacturers of industrial goods are more likely to use outsiders.

Sub-contracting is also a function of size, with a strong tendency for larger companies to use external agencies, especially marked in the case of marketing research.

C.5. ADVERTISING AND PROMOTION

Our study examined the extent to which firms having different characteristics employ various forms of promotion in their marketing programmes. As may be seen from Table C.6, the most common form of promotional activity was personal selling, used by 90 per cent of all firms.

TABLE C.6 *Use of Specific Forms of Promotion*

N = 553

	%
Personal Selling	90
Exhibitions	71
Above-the-line Advertising	65
Public Relations	57
Direct Mail	57
Below-the-line Promotion	44
Others	23

Thus we see that almost all firms find it necessary to confront their customers personally, although, in the case of consumer goods, they will rarely be the ultimate customers, in order to promote the availability and sale of their products. When we consider other forms of promotional activity, it is surprising to discover the high incidence of exhibitions – used by seven out of ten of all firms. As we might expect, the extent to which these are used varies according to the nature of the firm's principal business activity and these differences are discussed below. Nevertheless, it is worth noting here that even amongst manu-

104 ORGANIZATIONAL DESIGN FOR MARKETING FUTURES

facturers of consumer goods, exhibitions were only marginally less common than above-the-line advertising as elements in the promotional programme. Above-the-line advertising is in fact the next most common form of promotion and is important enough to be used by two-thirds of all firms.

Thus, personal selling, exhibitions and above-the-line advertising are the principal types of promotional activity found in our largest companies. Basically, therefore, the external manifestations of marketing activity have not changed inherently since the 1930s, when personal selling and advertising were established as the main weapons in the commercial struggle. Naturally, the form of these activities has changed greatly. Above-the-line advertising has made telling use of new technology, particularly television, and the role of personal selling has changed, sometimes dramatically. The only other broad types of promotion that are used by over half of all firms are direct mail and public relations, each used by 57 per cent of companies. Direct mail has clearly become an established part of the marketing scene, providing the important facility of directing promotion to the target market segment. Somewhat surprisingly, other below-the-line promotions are not yet used by a majority of firms. Surprisingly, since competitions, trading stamps and premium offers have become part of the market environment. The explanation lies, of course, in the relatively low use of such below-the-line promotion by firms which are not marketing consumer goods. No other broad type of promotional method is in common use and indeed only one in four companies is using methods other than those reviewed above.

Naturally, only very few firms are relying simply on one method of promotion – slightly more than one in ten of all firms. The concept of the marketing mix pinpoints the need of most companies to achieve multiple objectives – for example, to create a favourable image amongst its various publics, to secure distribution channels for its goods, to obtain consumer trial of its products and, subsequently, to enjoy consumer loyalty. In order to achieve these multiple objectives, a many-pronged promotional strategy is required and the present study indicates that almost a third of all firms are using four distinctly different promotional methods (Table C.7). Of the remainder,

BRITISH MARKETING ORGANIZATIONAL STATUS QUO 105

TABLE C.7 *Number of Forms of Promotion Used*

N = 553

No. of forms of promotion used	%
One	12
Two	25
Three	25
Four	31
Five	4

most are involved in either two or three different types of activity, whilst not many firms are using more than five major types of promotion.

A closer examination of the overall picture shows some interesting differences according to the firm's size and its principal business activity. If we look first of all at this latter characteristic, we can sketch a pen-picture of the manufacturers of consumer goods, of industrial goods and so on. The firm whose main marketing efforts must be directed to the man or woman in the street is much more likely to use several forms of promotion. Three out of four firms in this position use at least three methods, thus underlining the greater complexity of their marketing tasks. The types of methods used in this situation will also be different from the general pattern. Above-the-line advertising, below-the-line promotions and public relations will be more common, whereas direct mail and personal selling are less common. If, on the other hand, the firm is manufacturing goods for industrial or institutional customers, it is more likely that only two or three broad types of promotion will be used and the firm will rely more than its counterpart in the consumer field on personal selling, direct mail and exhibitions. It will thus direct its flow of information and persuasion in a much more concentrated fashion. Nevertheless, other forms of promotion are not uncommon amongst industrial producers, with above-the-line advertising used by over 60 per cent and public relations by half of firms in this group.

The remaining two groups of business activity which were examined – distributors and service industries – are less amenable to these rather general statements than manufacturers. However, it is apparent that firms in both groups are likely to use fewer methods of promotion. Both groups are, nonetheless, more likely to use direct mail promotion, though less likely

106 ORGANIZATIONAL DESIGN FOR MARKETING FUTURES

than manufacturers to use other methods; this tendency is most marked in the case of below-the-line promotion and exhibitions.

The use of several types of promotion is also strongly related to the firm's size. Whereas 28 per cent of companies in the smallest size group by turnover are using only one promotional method and only a small minority more than three methods, hardly any firms in the largest size groups rely only on one method and well over half are using at least three methods. Once again, we see how the complexity of the firm's tasks increases with its size. Likewise, there are important differences in the nature of this promotional activity. Smaller firms are particularly less likely to run either above-the-line or below-the-line campaigns, or to organize a formal public relations function. However, they are just as likely as their larger counterparts to rely on personal selling, and they take part in exhibitions to only a slightly less pronounced extent. The necessity of organizing and managing personal selling activities is universal and the difference in the nature of promotional tasks between small and large firms lies largely in the latter's more frequent use of mass-communication methods.

The decision as to how much finance should be allocated for promotional expenditure is traditionally one of the most difficult tasks in the marketing area. We examined first of all the end result of this decision-making process in terms of the proportion of direct sales revenue that firms allocate to their promotional activities. The great majority – four in five – of all firms allocate less than 10 per cent of their gross sales revenue to this end and almost half of all firms spend less than 3 per cent of GSR. A breakdown of results from all firms is contained in Table C.8.

TABLE C.8 *Proportion of Gross Sales Revenue allocated to Promotional Expenditure*

N = 553

% of Sales Revenue	%
Below 1%	25
1%–2.9%	23
3%–4.9%	19
5%–10%	15
Over 10%	9

As we see, only approximately one in ten firms is spending more than 10 per cent of its income from sales on advertising and promotion. However, manufacturers as a whole and particularly those operating in consumer goods markets, allocate a higher proportion of their revenue to promotion than do distributors and firms providing services. Thirty-five per cent of consumer goods manufacturers spend a proportion of 5 per cent or more of GSR whereas well over half of firms in the distributive and service categories are spending less than 3 per cent. This reflects the relative differences in the tasks to be performed and highlights the fact that, generally speaking, manufacturers must pay higher regard to their promotional efforts in relation to their total activities. No such clear pattern emerges, however, if we examine promotional expenditure in relation to the size of the firm. For example, more than half of the firms in the smallest but one size category, and firms in the two largest size groups spend less than 3 per cent. At the other end of the scale, there is a somewhat clearer tendency for fewer firms in the largest size groups to spend more than 5 per cent of GSR on promotion. Thus, as a general rule, firms tend to allocate a somewhat lower proportion of their revenues to advertising and promotion as their size increases.

As we said earlier, this proportion represents only the end result of a difficult decision. The difficulty is due in no small measure to the lack of sound procedures which might enable marketing management to evaluate the effectiveness of promotional activity. Some broad guidelines exist which might save the firm from expenditure which is too excessive, yet do not permit the identification of an optimal budget size. The present research has shown clearly that the old maxims of 'spend what we can afford' or 'spend what we spent last year' have given way to new foundations for decision making. Thus, it is heartening to discover that over half of all firms are basing their calculations either on the basis of expected future sales or the firm's needs or objectives (Table C.9).

In the case of most firms basing calculations on expected future sales, some methodical consideration of the future is implicit – in the latter cost considerations of need or objectives must be matched by an attempt to evaluate the cost-effectiveness of the promotional programmes designed. Quite what form these

108   ORGANIZATIONAL DESIGN FOR MARKETING FUTURES

TABLE C.9 *Basis for Determining Advertising Appropriation*

N = 553

	%
Proportion of Expected Future Sales	39
Analysis of Needs of Objectives	19
Proportion of Past Sales	11
Proportion of Profit	7
Historical Expenditure	2
As much as can be Afforded	1

considerations take in the firms concerned has not been established on a quantitative basis, although there is good reason for believing that in many cases firms are employing a relatively stringent methodological framework such as that offered by modern decision theory procedures. Of the other bases which were reported for determining the advertising appropriations, only the calculation of a proportion of past sales or, perhaps more promisingly, past profit were of any significance. However, approximately one in five firms were unable to give an answer to this part of the study and it is inferred that the informal and highly subjective nature of decision processes traditionally found continues in many firms. Once again, differences are present between firms of varying characteristics. Thus, manufacturers and distributors are more likely to base their methods on an analysis of needs and objectives than firms in service industries. Smaller firms are more likely to use a base of historical sales whereas the tendency to base decision making on needs or objectives increases with a firm's size.

C.6. PRICING

The task of setting prices for a firm's product or service has, once again, been traditionally regarded as demanding a decision process which does not lend itself to formalization. The way in which a firm arrives at its pricing structures can, it has been suggested, reflect its degree of orientation in the market place. Certainly it is possible to adopt an approach of measuring the costs of production, taking into account direct and all indirect costs, then adding an appropriate margin for a contribution to the firm's profit and advertising. This seems to be a somewhat redundant method for most firms – in our study only

BRITISH MARKETING ORGANIZATIONAL STATUS QUO

one in ten of the total adopted this general approach. Many firms – approximately a quarter of the total – are using as a starting point for their pricing the conditions that obtain in the market, whether they be the competitive environment or the acceptability of a price to the customer. At some stage, of course, cost considerations must enter into the deliberations of these firms, otherwise in the long run they will not survive. Nonetheless, the fact that so many of the firms studied consider their pricing to depend solely on market conditions indicates the progress that the approach of market-oriented pricing has made. The great majority of firms report explicitly that their prices are a result of establishing the costs and then modifying their calculations by an assessment of market conditions. Manufacturers are less likely to adopt a simple 'cost-plus' approach than firms in other groups. They will more frequently adopt a market-oriented approach. The tendency to introduce market considerations also increases strongly with the size of firm.

C.7. DISTRIBUTION CHANNELS

The nature of the distribution channels selected by a company depends substantially on the nature of its activity. The logic of firms who are industrial producers and have relatively few customers having shorter channels of distribution is evidenced in the present study.

As far as the total sample was concerned, the following distribution channels were used:

TABLE C.10 *Distribution Channels Used*

N = 553

	%
Direct to Users	41
Wholesalers and Retailers	26
Wholesalers Only	13
Retailers Only	11
Others	9

Thus, the most common style for a firm was for it to distribute directly to its customers without using any intermediary. This is largely accounted for by the very common occurrence of this situation amongst producers of industrial goods, as shown in Table C.11.

110 ORGANIZATIONAL DESIGN FOR MARKETING FUTURES

TABLE C.11 *Distribution Channels Used*

N = 278

Industrial Goods Producers

	%
Direct to Users	69
Wholesalers and Retailers	5
Wholesalers Only	15
Retailers Only	4
Others	7

If we look, however, at manufacturers of consumer goods, we find a very different pattern. In this situation, manufacturers will normally use a combination of wholesale and retailer intermediaries and only in a very small minority of cases will they distribute directly to their final customers (Table C.12).

TABLE C.12 *Distribution Channels Used*

N = 190

Consumer Goods Producers

	%
Direct to Users	6
Wholesalers and Retailers	62
Wholesalers Only	12
Retailers Only	18
Others	2

Although the length of the firm's distribution channel is largely determined by the main nature of its business activity, it is also possible to discover a relationship between a firm's size and the complexity of distribution channels, which generally increases with the size of firm.

C.8. SALES FORECASTING

The following section contains the evidence which we have obtained on the firm's need to look ahead to the future, specifically by producing forecasts of its sales for a given period ahead. Our survey established the sales forecasting horizon, in that we obtained indications of the furthest periods ahead for which firms are forecasting. Clearly, a firm that is forecasting sales for over five years in the future will also be making estimates of the situation in the much shorter term, such as the

BRITISH MARKETING ORGANIZATIONAL STATUS QUO

TABLE C.13 *Length of Sales Forecasting Period*

	%
N = 553	
Time Period	
Less than One Year	18
1–3 Years	51
3–5 Years	17
5–10 Years	13
10 Years and Over	1

next twelve months. Table C.13 contains the results for all firms in the study.

It is very interesting to note that a great majority of firms report that sales forecasts are prepared for periods further away than the next twelve months.

Half of all firms are in fact forecasting for between one and three years ahead although our qualitative research suggests that many of these will be at the shorter end of the scale. Nevertheless, an important minority of firms – one in three – is going beyond the three-year horizon up to five or ten years into the future. Ten years appears to be the virtual limit for forecasting sales.

As we might expect, certain differences are found amongst firms with different characteristics. Manufacturers as a whole tend to have longer horizons than other firms, although there is a very similar pattern for manufacturers of both consumer goods and industrial goods. The main differences occur on the dimension of company size, where larger companies clearly tend to forecast further ahead into the future.

C.9. WRITTEN-DOWN MARKETING PLANS

We regarded this as a key element in our investigation. Marketing activities without the discipline of planning can quickly become an unco-ordinated and inefficient series of tactics usually in response to environmental conditions in the market – competitive action, innovation, etc. The firm which is setting out to plan its marketing activities will almost certainly derive a more substantial advantage from future developments – which may be partly of its own making – than the firm which is merely reacting to events. Although, of course, virtually every

112 ORGANIZATIONAL DESIGN FOR MARKETING FUTURES

firm will be looking into the future in some way, as evidenced by the above findings on sales forecasting, we are concerned here with examining the extent to which plans are formally developed and committed to paper. Such plans can be communicated within the organization and represent a form of control on future performance. We are also concerned with the nature of such plans.

Overall, the existence of written-down marketing plans was reported by 56 per cent of the respondent firms. Thus, almost half of all firms are not committing themselves to formal planning in this important area. If we consider company size, a strong relationship is found. Virtually all firms in the largest size category develop plans of this kind, whereas less than one in four of the smallest firms do so. Manufacturers of consumer goods are slightly more committed to plans and manufacturers as a whole have written-down plans more commonly than other firms.

When we examine the length of the planning period within those firms which report the existence of written-down plans, we find a picture that corresponds very closely with that found earlier in the case of sales forecasting horizons (Table C.14).

TABLE C.14 *Length of Planning Period*

N = 307 (All firms with plans)	%
Less than One Year	18
One and up to Three Years	56
Three Years and up to Five Years	14
Five Years to Ten Years	12

Thus, the planning period is most commonly a period between one and three years ahead and very few firms have what might be considered a long-range marketing planning horizon. This is particularly true for manufacturers of consumer goods who either feel less need to plan for a long period ahead or find it impossible to do so reliably. On the other hand, two in every five producers of industrial goods were planning ahead for periods in excess of three years. However, no clear relationship exists between firms of different characteristics and the length of the planning period, given that firms in the smallest size categories have plans much more rarely.

BRITISH MARKETING ORGANIZATIONAL STATUS QUO 113

Although it is difficult to examine the contents of these plans in detail in a sample of such size, we have been able to identify the main sections of the plans which were reported and the incidence of certain key headings is reported in Table C.15.

TABLE C.15 *Content of Marketing Plans*

N = 553

	%
Analysis of Present Situation	12
Objectives	27
Profit/financial Plans	12
Diversification/innovation Plans	11
Promotional Strategy	25
Other Sections	23
No Response	21
Not Applicable	37

This table is based on the full sample and the high level of non-response partly reflects the number of firms who do not possess written-down marketing plans but also indicates that some firms who claim to have such plans are in fact unable to report any specific features about them. Thus, we may have over-recorded the incidence of marketing plans.

As to what we expected to find in marketing plans, we should certainly be looking for some form of appraisal of the present situation, a statement of future objectives – including financial plans – and some indication of the strategies to be employed to meet these objectives, such as promotional activity and plans for diversification and innovation.

As we see from Table C.15, only slightly more than one in ten firms in our sample are committing an analysis of the present situation to a marketing plan document, and only approximately one in four firms is putting its objectives and plans for promotional activity on paper. As far as innovation/diversification and financial plans are concerned, these are written down even less frequently. The implications of this situation are open to interpretation but it might be the case that only a minority of firms know at all clearly where they want to go and how to get there. On the other hand, it is possible that senior management has in many firms a relatively clear view of its objectives and strategies but is reluctant to commit these to paper or to communicate them down through the company.

H

114   ORGANIZATIONAL DESIGN FOR MARKETING FUTURES

C.10.   ORGANIZING FOR MARKETING RESEARCH

a. The Development of Marketing Research in the United Kingdom

The study which we are reporting here examined in some detail the current pattern of marketing research activities in British industry. Although these results have in themselves great relevance for our understanding of this important sphere of marketing activity, they become more valuable if we place them in their proper historical perspective.

Unfortunately very little information has been obtained on the early development of marketing research in the United Kingdom. The study which is most frequently referred to was limited by its narrow approach to the whole field and particularly by its small sample. Nevertheless, it is worth looking briefly at its principal findings. The study was carried out on behalf of the British Institute of Management and was published as their Information Summary No. 97. Its findings were based on information received from eighty-six companies on their marketing research activities during 1960 which included representatives of the principal industrial groups and advertising agencies. The study can not be considered as representative of the overall situation but, nevertheless, it does give us an impression of the situation. In order to make these results more useful for our analysis of the present situation, a small study was carried out amongst the firms that co-operated in the earlier study, which asked for exactly the same information on the firms' marketing research activities in 1968. Although only fifty-seven firms eventually co-operated in this second survey, the findings did suggest that during the intervening period quite substantial growth was occurring in the marketing research industry. Fourteen of the fifty-seven firms had established marketing research departments during the period and in 1968 only a very small proportion had no internal department of their own. The amounts spent on marketing research have increased, with an average of £65,000 spent by each firm in 1968 compared to £35,000 in 1960. Growth in average expenditure was particularly marked in manufacturers of consumer goods, whereas industrial goods producers showed an average increase of 30 per cent on the 1960 base. The proportion of total expenditure represented by work commissioned externally has increased and the average number of staff employed within marketing research departments has shown a fall from seventeen to thirteen.

As far as the organizational aspects are concerned, there is a strong indication that the structures for the research function are in a state of flux. Many firms report that they have reorganized or are currently reorganizing their arrangements. In particular, there is a trend away from the single, central, marketing research division to a pattern which incorporates a central department but also smaller divisional departments, particularly amongst producers of industrial goods. The importance of corporate planning as a business orientation appears to demand a central service, particularly for forecasting and new product development whereas the specialist needs of divisional or departmental operating groups are frequently seen to justify a specialist marketing research service.

Interesting findings emerge on the extent to which it is believed that recommendations are acted upon by management – over half of the firms investigated indicate that such recommendations are followed only occasionally; the greatest pessimists are to be found amongst manufacturers of industrial goods.

Looking now outside the context of this small-scale survey, a number of more general points need to be made about the development of marketing research in the United Kingdom. Growth in the number of firms who establish their marketing decisions at least partially on a base of marketing information has been continuous and is particularly marked in the industrial sector, as evidenced for example in the growth of the Industrial Market Research Association (IMRA). As we shall see below, our study of marketing in 553 companies indicated that over two-thirds of the firms in this group do carry out marketing research of some kind. It is therefore suggested that the future will not see such a large increase in the numbers of firms who are active in the area of marketing research. Developments are much more likely to arise in the ways that firms organize their systems for obtaining, processing and utilizing their information. The term 'marketing information system' is now used to describe the sort of situation where these activities are regularized into a continuous operation, permitting the

116 ORGANIZATIONAL DESIGN FOR MARKETING FUTURES

firm to be much more aware of the changes in the market. At present, much information is obtained on a somewhat haphazard *ad hoc* basis to meet specific needs which management has identified. It is likely that sophisticated marketing information systems will become much more common, although it is difficult at the present time to find more than a handful of firms which have designed and implemented such systems in the United Kingdom. However, such speculation must be examined in the light of the evidence on current practice which we report below.

b. The Current Status of Marketing Research

Our evidence here is based on information supplied by the 553 firms during our major study of marketing activities and organization structures. Clearly, not all firms will carry out marketing research and we established initially which firms qualified for the investigation into the kinds of information which they acquire, and the organizational aspects of their data-collecting activities. As we seen from Table C.16, 74 per cent of all firms report that they do carry out marketing research at least occasionally.

Amongst manufacturers of consumer goods, four in every

TABLE C.16 *Whether Marketing Research Ever Carried Out by Nature of Business Activity*

	No. of Firms	% Carrying Out Marketing Research
Total	553	74
Manufacturers of Consumer Goods	189	80
Manufacturers of Industrial Goods	278	75
Distributors	40	60
Service Industries	28	50
Others	18	56

by Turnover

	No. of Firms	% Carrying Out Marketing Research
Total	553	74
Below £1 m.	57	47
£1 m.–4.9 m.	257	71
£5 m.–9.9 m.	96	79
£10 m.–24.9 m.	66	86
£25 m.–49.9 m.	27	100
£50 m.–& over	19	100
Turnover not Established	31	61

BRITISH MARKETING ORGANIZATIONAL STATUS QUO   117

five firms are carrying out marketing research. Larger firms are much more likely to be active in this area, as are those companies whose chief marketing executive has the title of marketing director or marketing manager (90 per cent in each case).

Thus it is established that the vast majority of firms of a certain minimum size – whose turnover exceeds £1 million – do at some time commission and use marketing research. However, the majority of these user firms have not in fact appointed a full-time executive to be responsible for marketing research. A smaller proportion of all companies has in fact made such an appointment, since some firms are not in fact carrying out any marketing research. (See Table C.17.)

TABLE C.17 *Whether Full-time Executive Appointed for Marketing Research by Nature of Business Activity*

	No. of Firms	% of firms who have appointed full-time executive for marketing research
Total	553	28
Manufacturers of Consumer Goods	189	32
Manufacturers of Industrial Goods	278	30
Distributors	40	8
Service Industries	28	11
Others	18	33

by Turnover

	No. of Firms	% of firms who have appointed full-time executive for marketing research
Total	553	28
Below £1 million	57	0
£1 m.–4.9 m.	257	20
£5 m.–9.9 m.	96	36
£10 m.–24.9 m.	66	43
£25 m.–49.9 m.	27	55
£50 m.–over	19	89
Turnover not Established	31	27

The proportion of firms which have a full-time executive is higher amongst manufacturers and increases substantially with turnover. Thus, no firm with a turnover below £1 million possesses a full-time marketing research executive, although

118   Organizational Design for Marketing Futures

they are found in a majority of the firms with a turnover exceeding £25 million.

Of the 162 firms who have a full-time executive, the majority report that the appointment was first made more than three years before. The full figures on the timing of appointment are shown in Table C.18.

Table C.18 *Appointment of Full-time Marketing Research Executive*

N = 162

Full Time Appointment Made	%
Less than One Year Ago	13
One Year and Less than Three Years Ago	30
Three Years and Less than Five Years Ago	20
Five Years and Less than Ten Years Ago	23
Ten Years or More Ago	14

The replication of the original BIM study on Marketing Research in British Industry showed that the peak time for establishing a marketing research department was between 1956 and 1962–4. If we compare these findings, then it is clear that the sample for the smaller study was relatively more advanced in instituting a formal department than in our major study.

c. Designations of Marketing Research Executives

Where full-time executives had been appointed, a variety of titles are given. The most common were market research manager (32 per cent) and market research officer (19 per cent). The former was more general amongst manufacturers of consumer goods, whilst amongst industrial goods producers, a quarter designated him market research manager, a quarter market research officer and the remaining 50 per cent of firms gave him a different title.

The majority of these marketing research executives (71 per cent) have written-down job descriptions.

d. Responsibility for Marketing Research Executives

Still considering those firms who carry out marketing research, we find that responsibility for supervising the activity of the senior marketing research executive is more commonly located with the marketing director or marketing manager, or, in a fifth of cases, with the chief executive. Many firms have not allocated supervisory responsibility to any specific individual.

Some interesting differences in the allocation of responsibility may be found if we examine firms operating in different business situations. Thus, it is equally common amongst manufacturers of industrial goods to find the marketing research manager reporting to the sales director as to the marketing director. This clearly reflects the extent to which the sales director is the chief marketing executive in such companies. Firms in the largest size groups have their marketing research staff reporting more commonly to a marketing director.

e. Expenditure on Marketing Research

Marketing research agencies are, naturally, concerned with establishing the size of the market for their services. However, in view of the essentially clandestine nature of such activities and the problems of definition concerned, satisfactory estimates have rarely been produced. The replicated BIM study, referred to earlier, reports that the total expenditure on marketing research by fifty-seven companies amounts to £3,210,000, of which £1,896,000 was contracted to external agencies in 1968. The *average* expenditure per firm was £65,500. On the basis that the estimated turnover of the companies concerned was £3,612.5 million and the total turnover of UK manufacturing industry in 1968 was £36,686 million a rough estimate of total expenditure on marketing research in the UK was made of £32 million per annum. The mean expenditure of the companies in our sample was much lower – those who carry out marketing research and answered the relevant question produced a mean expenditure of approximately £20,000. Nevertheless, the firms in this sample represent approximately one-seventh of total turnover and their total expenditure was in the region of £4.5 million. A simple calculation of total expenditure thus yields a figure also in the region of £30 million. This is so much in excess of conventional estimates that its validity must be questioned and reasons are not difficult to find. We might hypothesize, for example, that non-respondents spend less on marketing research. Thus our estimate of total expenditure may be below £30 million but is probably well in excess of the conventional estimates of around £18 million.

Having performed these subjective mathematical exercises, we can examine the extent to which the individual enterprise

120 ORGANIZATIONAL DESIGN FOR MARKETING FUTURES

TABLE C.19 *Expenditure on Marketing Research*

N = 408 (all firms who carry out marketing research)

Amount spent in last financial year £'s	%
Up to 9,999	33
10,000–19,999	10
20,000–29,999	4
30,000–39,999	2
40,000–49,999	1
50,000–59,999	2
60,000–99,999	1
100,000 or more	2
No response	45

is committing its resources to marketing research. Table C.19 contains the results from our study and the first point to highlight is the high level of non-response. This appeared to be partly caused by reluctance to publish the relevant figures, but is also partly explained by the inability of the firm to calculate its true level of expenditure.

No firm in the lowest turnover group, below £1 million, spent more than £10,000 in its last financial year whereas, at the other end of the scale, almost half of the firms in the largest turnover group spent in excess of £20,000. Manufacturers of consumer goods are relatively high spenders: their figures are shown in Table C.20 along with their counterparts in industrial markets:

TABLE C.20 *Expenditure on Marketing Research*

£'s	Consumer Goods N = 151 %	Industrial Goods N = 209 %
Up to 9,999	17	35
10,000–19,999	13	7
20,000–29,999	5	4
30,000–39,999	5	0
40,000–49,999	1	0
50,000–59,999	4	1
60,000–99,999	1	0
100,000 or more	3	0
No response	51	47

The two firms in industrial markets who are spending over £50,000 are therefore completely out on their own.

f. Profile of Marketing Research Activities

In addition to discovering which conventional marketing research activities were being performed by the firms which we investigated, we also set out to establish whether or not some form of test marketing procedure had ever been used. Our implied definition of this activity was a launch in a restricted geographical area designed to test new products. Overall, only 30 per cent of all firms have used such a procedure, although approximately 50 per cent of all manufacturers of consumer goods have tested at least one of their new products in this way. Perhaps, more surprisingly, in view of the lack of facilities which exists and also the difficulties of controlling tests in an industrial situation, as many as one in five of industrial goods producers claimed to have done some test marketing in the past. This would appear to contradict the conventional viewpoint that test marketing operations are rarely if ever conducted by a manufacturer of industrial goods.

As far as the mainstream of marketing research activity is concerned, the findings for all companies are contained in Table C.21.

This represents a report of those activities which are ever carried out, and to what extent they are carried out by internal personnel, external agencies or both. With the exception of retail audits, research into special offers and advertising copy research, a majority of firms reported activity in every sphere. Those areas which were more widely investigated included sales analysis, studies of new product acceptability and the comparative performance of new products versus competition. It appears that external agencies are most commonly used in conjunction with internal resources; only in the case of copy research and media studies do they appear to be commonly used alone. Studies of product performance and new product acceptability and potential were carried out by internal and external facilities more commonly than other exercises. Research designed to establish sales quotas or to define sales territories appeared to be contracted externally by only a small minority of firms.

The concluding part of our investigation into marketing research activities concerned the extent to which certain parts of

122 ORGANIZATIONAL DESIGN FOR MARKETING FUTURES

TABLE C.21 *Areas of Marketing Research Activities*

N = 408	Not Carried Out	Carried Out Internally	Carried Out Externally	Carried Out Both Internally and Externally
	%	%	%	%
Studies of Acceptability and Potential of New Products	15	48	6	24
Studies of Present Products v. Competition	13	56	7	17
Packaging Research	41	23	6	11
Research on Competitors' Products	21	53	4	9
Product Testing, Blind Product Tests	34	33	6	11
Assessment of Market Potential	13	52	6	16
Determination of Market Characteristics	18	45	8	16
Market Share Analysis	13	53	11	16
Studies of Market Changes	30	37	9	12
Sales Analysis	6	79	1	9
Establishment of Sales Quotas	24	65	—	3
Establishment of Sales Territories	21	67	1	3
Studies of Effectiveness of Salesman Remuneration	39	43	2	8
Analysis of Effectiveness of Channels of Distribution	40	39	2	7
Distribution Cost Studies	35	46	2	5
Test Marketing	51	22	2	11
Retail Audits	65	6	9	5
Measuring Effectiveness of Special Offers	61	15	2	5
Copy Research	58	9	12	7
Media Studies	49	12	17	9

the marketing mix, for example the product, promotion and distribution, accounted for the total expenditure and the relative levels of use of the various alternative techniques. Unfortunately many firms found it difficult to report these breakdowns of their total activity and we are left with a fragmentary picture of the importance of the areas of research and the principal techniques.

For this reason, it is extremely difficult to make comparisons between firms having different types of business activity and between firms of differing size. We have confined ourselves therefore to global statements. The findings are contained in Tables C.22 to C.26.

Thus, in Table C.22, 4 per cent of firms allocated between

BRITISH MARKETING ORGANIZATIONAL STATUS QUO 123

TABLE C.22 *Proportions of Total Expenditure Allocated to Product Research*

N = 408 Proportion of Expenditure %	% of Firms
0– 9	2
10– 19	8
20– 29	9
30– 39	4
40– 49	5
50– 59	8
60– 69	2
70– 79	3
80– 89	2
90–100	2

TABLE C.23 *Proportions of Total Expenditure Allocated to Research into Market*

N = 408 Proportion of Expenditure %	% of Firms
0– 9	2
10– 19	4
20– 29	10
30– 39	5
40– 49	6
50– 59	8
60– 69	4
70– 79	2
80– 89	2
90–100	2

TABLE C.24 *Proportion of Total Expenditure Allocated to Sales and Distribution Research*

N = 408 Proportion of Expenditure %	% of Firms
0– 9	7
10– 19	5
20– 29	7
30– 39	3
40– 49	3
50– 59	3
60– 69	1
70– 79	—
80– 89	—
90–100	1

124   ORGANIZATIONAL DESIGN FOR MARKETING FUTURES

TABLE C.25 *Proportion of Total Expenditure Allocated to Advertising and Promotion Research*

N = 408

Proportion of Expenditure %	% of Firms
0– 9	—
10– 19	12
20– 29	5
30– 39	1
40– 49	1
50– 59	1
60– 69	1
70– 79	1
80– 89	3
90–100	11

TABLE C.26 *Proportion of Total Expenditure Allocated to Other Areas*

N = 408

Proportion of Expenditure %	% of Firms
0– 9	8
10–19	4
20–29	1

N.B. No other area accounted for a greater proportion of total expenditure than 30 per cent in any firm.

30 per cent and 39 per cent of their total budget to research into their products, whereas only two per cent of firms allocated between 90 per cent and 100 per cent of their expenditure in this area.

It would be dangerous to put too stringent an interpretation on these findings. Broadly speaking, however, there is a tendency for larger parts of the total budget to be devoted to product and market, as opposed to *marketing* research, whereas research into distribution and advertising and promotion tends to receive a lower proportion of the total, except in the case of advertising agencies who, not surprisingly, concentrate their expenditure in the sphere of advertising research. This accounts for the relatively high proportion of firms who allocate all or virtually all of their expenditure in this area.

If we look now at the proportions of the total budget which are distributed between the various technical alternatives, such as trade/retail audits, *ad hoc* surveys etc., a somewhat clearer

TABLE C.27 *Proportion of Marketing Research Allocated to Techniques*

Proportion of Expenditure	Qualitative Research	Trade/ Retail Audits	Customer Panels	Continuous Surveys	*Ad hoc* Surveys	Experi- mentation
% N =	408	408	408	408	408	408
0– 9	4	3	5	3	4	6
10–19	7	2	5	4	8	7
20–29	6	5	2	5	10	4
30–39	4	2	2	4	4	2
40–49	1	1	—	3	2	1
50–59	1	4	1	3	3	—
60–69	2	1	—	1	2	—
70–79	1	1	1	1	2	—
80–89	1	—	—	—	2	—
90–99	—	—	—	2	5	—

126 ORGANIZATIONAL DESIGN FOR MARKETING FUTURES

picture emerges. The overall results are contained in Table C.27.

Table C.27 should be read in the following terms. Looking at the Customer Panels heading, for example, 5 per cent of all firms allocate up to 9 per cent of their total budget to research which requires this technique. A further 5 per cent of firms allocate between 10 and 19 per cent of their total budget to this technique and so on.

Broadly speaking, we can see that more firms allocate the whole of their budget to *ad hoc* surveys than to any other type of technique. Qualitative research – such as group discussions and depth interviews – account usually for a relatively small proportion of the total, as do trade/retail audits and customer panels.

Experimental exercises, such as test marketing, rarely receive more than 20 per cent of the total budget on a formal basis, but since many firms find it difficult to allocate the incurred costs effectively it might well be the case that we are under-recording the proportionate allocations to this group of techniques.

If we were to summarize our findings on the present status of marketing research activities in British industry, we might point to the widespread acceptance of the need for marketing research in specific contexts but also to the relatively patchy commitment shown by most firms. They do not establish a full-time executive, for example, and are somewhat more committed to carrying out internal analyses than applying difficult techniques in the still important spheres of packaging, copy, media and below-the-line promotion.

C.11 MARKETING ATTITUDES AND DEFINITIONS

The final part of our investigation was concerned to probe the attitudes prevalent in respondent firms to the marketing concept orientation. In this section we present our findings in this respect, and attempt to reconcile these with the reported facts of the firm's activities and institutions.

At the outset we must emphasize our own keen awareness of the severe limitations of endeavours such as ours to research attitudes, particularly on a postal basis. Nevertheless, we believed that it was worthwhile to attempt this difficult task, especially since the folkloric tradition has hitherto given the strong impression that a very high proportion of our managements – even in the largest companies – are rooted in the eras of sales, or even product, orientation.

Our own experience in probing the attitudes of management towards the marketing concept was gained substantially during a programme of doctoral research by one of the associated co-authors of this study, Dr S. Saddik.* In the course of his industrially more limited study, it was discovered that managers in the industries concerned were almost equally divided between those who expressed favourable and unfavourable attitudes towards the marketing concept. The series of statements with which respondents in the present study were invited to disagree or agree were mainly derived from this earlier research. As in the rest of the study, the responses received were in the most part from the company's chief executive and it is therefore important to note that we are not here examining the attitudes of marketing specialists, which we might expect to have been even more favourable towards the marketing concept than those reported here.

First of all, we present the results for the total series of statements, showing the reaction of the total sample of 553 and the attitudes expressed by executives in the separate groups of firms stratified by the nature of their principal activity. Interpretation of these findings follows the full set of tables.

* Saddik, S. *Marketing in the Wool Textile, Textile Machinery and Clothing Industries.* Doctoral thesis, University of Bradford, 1969.

TABLE C.28 *Attitudes to the Statement: 'The marketing man's job is simply to sell what the works produce'*

Nature of Business Activity: Response to statement	Manuf. of Consumer Products 189 %	Manuf. of Industrial Products 278 %	Distribution 40 %	Services 28 %	Not Identified 18 %	All Companies 553 %
Strongly Agree	1	1	—	4	—	1
Agree	6	9	10	14	11	8
Undecided	0	1	23	4	6	1
Disagree	29	33	33	25	17	31
Strongly Disagree	62	54	39	35	49	55
No Response	2	2	15	18	17	4

TABLE C.29 *Attitudes to the Statement: 'Our main task is to increase Sales Volume. Profits will follow naturally'*

Nature of Business Activity: Response to statement	Manuf. of Consumer Products 189 %	Manuf. of Industrial Products 278 %	Distribution 40 %	Services 28 %	Not Identified 18 %	All Companies 553 %
Strongly Agree	2	3	—	7	11	3
Agree	9	15	23	25	17	14
Undecided	7	2	3	4	—	4
Disagree	46	43	42	31	22	43
Strongly Disagree	34	34	32	29	17	33
No Response	2	3	—	4	33	3

TABLE C.30 *Attitudes to the Statement: 'A well-made product will sell itself'*

Nature of Business Activity:	Manuf. of Consumer Products	Manuf. of Industrial Products	Distribution	Services	Not Identified	All Companies
Response to statement						
	189 %	278 %	40 %	28 %	18 %	553 %
Strongly Agree	1	1	—	—	—	1
Agree	8	8	2	18	6	10
Undecided	2	2	—	—	6	2
Disagree	58	64	62	60	38	61
Strongly Disagree	28	23	12	11	22	23
No Response	3	2	3	11	28	4

TABLE C.31 *Attitudes to the Statement: 'Further increases in profitability will be attained mainly by more efficient production'*

Nature of Business Activity:	Manuf. of Consumer Products	Manuf. of Industrial Products	Distribution	Services	Not Identified	All Companies
Response to statement						
	189 %	278 %	40 %	28 %	18 %	553 %
Strongly Agree	4	5	—	4	11	4
Agree	26	35	25	29	22	30
Undecided	7	6	12	—	6	7
Disagree	43	38	38	56	39	41
Strongly Disagree	16	12	5	—	—	12
No Response	4	4	20	11	22	6

TABLE C.32 *Attitudes to the Statement: 'Diversification policies should build on existing company resources'*

Nature of Business Activity:	Manuf. of Consumer Products	Manuf. of Industrial Products	Distribution	Services	Not Identified	All Companies
	189	278	40	28	18	553
	%	%	%	%	%	%
Response to statement						
Strongly Agree	5	5	3	7	—	5
Agree	58	58	58	57	33	57
Undecided	16	10	8	14	17	13
Disagree	15	20	15	18	—	17
Strongly Disagree	2	3	3	—	—	2
No Response	4	4	13	4	50	6

TABLE C.33 *Attitudes to the Statement: 'Provided we succeed in selling a planned level of production, we should not be too concerned with trends in the total market'*

Nature of Business Activity:	Manuf. of Consumer Products	Manuf. of Industrial Products	Distribution	Services	Not Identified	All Companies
	189	278	40	28	18	553
	%	%	%	%	%	%
Response to statement						
Strongly Agree	—	—	3	4	—	—
Agree	3	5	3	4	—	4
Undecided	3	3	3	8	—	3
Disagree	54	56	63	52	22	55
Strongly Disagree	39	35	18	21	28	34
No Response	1	1	10	11	50	4

TABLE C.34 *Attitudes to the Statement: 'In our type of business we know the market too well to need marketing research'*

Nature of Business Activity:	Manuf. of Consumer Products	Manuf. of Industrial Products	Distribution	Services	Not Identified	All Companies
Responses to statement						
	189	278	40	28	18	553
	%	%	%	%	%	%
Strongly Agree	—	1	—	—	—	—
Agree	27	10	8	8	6	8
Undecided	5	7	22	4	12	7
Disagree	50	52	50	55	17	52
Strongly Disagree	35	28	15	29	22	29
No Response	3	2	5	4	43	4

TABLE C.35 *Attitudes to the Statement: 'The marketing man's job is simply to sell what the works produce'*

Gross Sales Revenue:	Below £1 m	£1 m– 4.9 m	£5 m– 9.9 m	£10 m– 24.9 m	£25 m– 49.9 m	£50 m or Over	Not Established	All Companies
Response to statement								
	57	257	94	68	27	19	31	553
	%	%	%	%	%	%	%	%
Strongly Agree	—	2	—	—	—	—	3	1
Agree	21	10	5	3	3	—	6	8
Undecided	2	2	1	1	—	—	3	1
Disagree	26	32	4	31	33	37	43	31
Strongly Disagree	40	52	64	61	64	58	35	55
No Response	11	2	6	3	—	5	10	4

132 ORGANIZATIONAL DESIGN FOR MARKETING FUTURES

Clearly, there is no 'right' or 'wrong' answer to all of these statements. Agreement or disagreement with many of the statements may, however, be taken to indicate an expression of sympathy with the relevance of the marketing concept. Even discounting the effect inevitably produced by those respondents who are simply recording what they feel to be the 'right' response to some statement, interesting differences emerge. Those statements which are relatively ambiguous allow us to gain an insight into orientation, and they reveal that manufacturers of consumer goods are somewhat more strongly oriented towards the implications of the marketing concept than their counterparts in the industrial producing situation. An exception to this is, of course, shown in responses to the final statement 'In our type of business we know the market too well to need marketing research,' where a higher proportion of consumer goods manufacturers agree with this somewhat arrogant statement. Differences are also found along the dimension of company size, with the largest companies showing very marked attachment to the marketing concept. Table C.35 gives an example of this tendency, in this case the responses to the statement: 'The marketing man's job is simply to sell what the works produce.'

Our overall conclusion might be that, even allowing for respondents who report what they believe they should, the responses suggest a high level of expressed orientation towards the philosophy and the implications of the marketing concept. One or two contradictions remain. Thus, although 81 per cent of the total either disagreed or strongly disagreed with the statement that 'In our type of business we know the market too well to need marketing research', we found that only 74 per cent of firms are ever carrying out marketing research.

Further insight into the attitudes of respondents was obtained from the question which asked respondents what they understand by the term 'marketing'. This question naturally had the further purpose of attempting to probe levels of knowledge, although it became apparent that in some cases respondents had consulted with colleagues or even, in view of the suspiciously familiar nature of a few of the definitions presented, had taken recourse to one of the standard texts.

A selection of the actual replies to this question is provided as

British Marketing Organizational Status Quo 133

TABLE C.36 *Definitions of the term 'Marketing'*

N = 553

Summary of Definition:	%
Selling	13
Market Research	5
Advertising and Promotion	5
Having the right goods in the right place at the right time, at the right price – the 4 Rs.	3
Satisfaction of customer needs	14
Satisfaction of customer needs *profitably*	19
List of functions	9
The co-ordinative element in the firm	4
The total business operation	8
'Textbook' definitions e.g. Institute of Marketing	3
Not answered	17

Appendix 3 (p.209). However, we have attempted to summarize the content of all responses in Table C.36.

Thus, the largest group of responses contained reference to the satisfaction of customer needs and also the reservation that this should be achieved on a profitable basis, although the second largest group simply offered the social-conscious viewpoint of satisfying customer needs. Definitions which concentrated on regarding marketing as being synonymous with selling were common, whilst no other type of definition was given by more than 10 per cent of respondents. Some of these are significant, however, and some deserve further explanation. Market research, e.g., 'Identifying consumer needs', and advertising and promotion are straightforward and the three, or sometimes four, Rs approach is familiar enough. As far as function listing is concerned, 9 per cent of respondents felt it sufficient to recite selected elements of the marketing mix. Others, who saw marketing in an extreme light, regarded it as the element which co-ordinates all activities of the firm (4 per cent) or which simply constitutes the total business operation. Almost one in every five respondents felt unable to answer the question to his own satisfaction, but the results do by and large reveal sophisticated levels of knowledge concerning the marketing concept as a business philosophy and its operational implications, together with attitudes which are largely favourable to the marketing viewpoint. Somewhat surprisingly in view of other findings from this study, the generally satisfactory nature of responses reported above was received to a similar extent

134 ORGANIZATIONAL DESIGN FOR MARKETING FUTURES

from manufacturers of both consumer and industrial goods. Non-manufacturing firms did, however, show considerable variation from the basic pattern; for example, a relatively high proportion of distributors saw marketing as being synonymous with selling. It is difficult to identify a clear pattern in terms of company turnover. Although more firms in the smallest group defined marketing as 'selling', this also applied in the largest but one size category £25–49.9 million per annum turnover.

This then concludes our empirical analysis of the organizational *status quo* in British marketing. We shall now turn to ponder the problems of organizational transfer and development that arise if British marketing is to organize itself effectively for the tasks which lie in wait. This will be the content of Part D.

PART D

ORGANIZATIONAL TRANSFER –
ORGANIZATIONAL DEVELOPMENT

The chief marketing executive's main organizational assignment in the seventies must be to match the structure he commands to the tasks which lie before his company. In this part we shall explore some of the ways in which it seems that this assignment can be met. We shall be explicitly considering a series of vital dimensions of the marketing activity in line with the scenarios which we developed in Part A and our empirical findings reported in Part C.

The dimensions include most notably the routinization of most operational marketing activities and their analytical separation from the marketing development task of the business; the fusion of R & D planning activities with Marketing Development; the development of the customer service function in the business and of effective marketing intelligence systems; the stimulation of a total approach to the physical distribution of goods and services to markets; internationalization of structures; increasing attention to the educational development and training of staff at all levels; and, finally, the ethical and aesthetic elements of marketing's task.

We shall look at each of these dimensions in turn and then attempt to indicate ways in which the marketing organization can cope with their overall effective co-ordination and control.

D.I. THE ROUTINIZATION OF OPERATIONAL MARKETING ACTIVITIES

Routinization is something that the traditional marketer resists – he dubbs it bureaucracy which he normally associates with the financial area of the business. The routines with which marketing has hitherto been familiar are to a considerable

136 ORGANIZATIONAL DESIGN FOR MARKETING FUTURES

degree perceived as wasted – a frequently cited example is the sales visit or contact report which is laboriously prepared and filed carefully away. No cogent use is made of many such documents which are in any event perceived as something of a distraction by the aggressive man in the field. The annual planning exercise is sometimes seen in a somewhat similar light. Although the act of planning is enjoyable enough, the implementation of plans is less easily accomplished and considerably less agreeable. The temptation to oversell a line which is obviously in substantial demand, to a level which disrupts the planned activity, is hard to resist. The sheer hard work involved in boosting a flagging line to reach target is sometimes hard to muster.

The application of work study procedures and the implementation of new travel cycles which disrupt existing habit patterns, and go against personal convenience, are often eschewed. Such resistance is justified by senior marketing executives in an organization in the cause of encouraging initiative by allowing a maximum of discretion to the individual within the marketing function. Flair and the need for creativity in the advertising or public relations sector of the business is denied by none; equally so in the new product conception and development process for a company. But the encouragement of flair and creativity can become an excuse, and often does, for an almost total lack of analytical rigour in the development of such activities. It is not sufficient to have even the most brilliantly creative promotional campaign without that campaign moving in on the designated target market, and without the routinization of media planning and selection procedures. In the public relations field neither the indiscriminate lobbying of journalists or TV contributors and producers, nor the incessant bombardment of news desks with press releases, can be a substitute for the cogently thought-out strategy which is implicit in media planning and selection above-the-line.

The distribution area also suffers from a similar lack of routine analysis. Service levels are a classic example of the way in which externally-oriented marketing enthusiasm can substantially reduce corporate profitability when levels of 90 per cent or more at twenty-four hours are insisted upon by marketing executives. A more selective approach, and a thorough cost–

ORGANIZATIONAL TRANSFER – ORGANIZATIONAL DEVELOPMENT 137

benefit analysis are mundane but vital marketing routines for all businesses.

Marketing's problem, in identifying those areas where a routinized approach is necessary and can make a valuable contribution to effective future operations, surely lies in the nature of the marketing animal we have bred in the past decade. Much of this breeding has been incestuous – taking salesmen and technical staff from their professional field and calling upon them to change their nature, to change from being essentially creative men who live by their wits and inventiveness rather than by their capacity to grapple with analytical routine. Men or women with the inclination to go-it-alone, to make their own personal sale or develop their own personally improved technique or system are seldom ideally suited to the detailed planning and control procedures which must underpin the complex and sophisticated pattern of marketing activities in our large- and medium-sized enterprises. Of the two, the presently least preferred, that is the man with the technical background, is probably better equipped intellectually for the task in that he will have a strong scientific training in analytical methodology which will stand him in better marketing stead. Inevitably, however, the great majority of marketing men today are former salesmen whose experiential background will often militate against effective marketing performance.

The marketing man of the sixties can be caricatured as a corporate extrovert, seeking after opportunities rather than solving problems, and glorying in the chase after profitable sales volume. Inevitably, he fell down on an important part of his task and was a constant source of anxiety to colleagues elsewhere in the business – in the production and financial sectors in particular. He often exacerbated their problems of production scheduling and/or cash flow analysis. In truth, the marketing task of the seventies demands an organization which attends to the tribological problems of the marketing animal of the sixties, the marketing interface with production and finance, as well as the company interface with the customer. The assignment, the organizational need, will be hard to fulfil. Marketing's traditional authority in the firm is externally derived as the generator of the revenue flows for the business from

138 ORGANIZATIONAL DESIGN FOR MARKETING FUTURES

people, customers which only the marketers meet. To create a sense of inner directedness or introverted corporate responsibility within such an environment demands bold, skilled management and imaginative initiatives.

An analogy can perhaps usefully be drawn with the separation, even the divorce, of production management and research and development within many enterprises in the twenties and thirties. Historically, these two activities in the business were linked or joined together in one single departmental activity. The divergent nature of the tasks which were implicit in producing products to sell this week, month or year, and those implicit in a programme of pure basic or applied developmental research to ensure the company's future growth and success, ultimately forced an organizational separation. In some businesses, engineering development departments or units are present to ease the transition from R & D to the routine of production and delivery schedules, but at root an organizational separation has generally emerged. Are not the two elements in marketing's task diverging in such a way as to justify, even to demand, the organizational separation of 'Operational Marketing' and 'Marketing Development'? It is our contention that the seventies demand such a separation in the marketing area and that much of the corporate planning backlash against marketing has arisen because of marketing's failure to discern this need and to adopt the institutional structure by which the marketing task is traditionally accomplished.

In Figure D.1 we have identified what seem to be the critical tasks for operational marketing activity in the future. There is little to be seen which is new in conception; what we wish to emphasize is that a shift in balance is required, in favour of the routinization process to such an extent that the marketing man of the sixties must be excused if he proclaims our proposal as a charter for the bureaucrats. The powerful focus for operational effectiveness must be the department charged with the work of auditing and controlling the marketing activity as it unfolds during the current planning period. This is, of course, a much wider concept than the conventional budgetary control process with its analyses of variances of performance against target. It involves control on several additional dimensions within the marketing sphere to cover marketing costs in the

ORGANIZATIONAL TRANSFER – ORGANIZATIONAL DEVELOPMENT 139

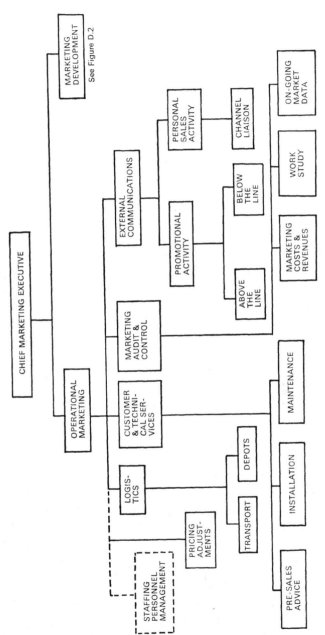

Figure D.1 OPERATIONAL MARKETING'S ORGANIZATIONAL TASKS

140 ORGANIZATIONAL DESIGN FOR MARKETING FUTURES

sales promotion and distribution sectors, as well as revenue flows. It encompasses the application in the short term of work study and measurement procedures within the office and without, and even more importantly, the variance between own and competitive performance. One of the major criticisms we can advance against the previous separation of budgetary control in the finance department and competitive market performance in a marketing department (in those firms where both tasks were in fact being undertaken), was that the total perspective on performance was not obtained. A marketing audit and control department or unit will be in the position to exercise this overall assessment and to bring about any adjustments to plans which *either* failure to meet own plans, *or* external competitive shortfall make necessary. The rapid response to gross market movement or individual competitive activity must in our contention be built right into the operational marketing activity. This inevitably involves the use of trade sales and stock audit procedures, user panels and the like as well as the analysis of internal company sales records.

Logistics is a routinized sector which we shall be discussing in considerable detail in Section D.5 where the implications of total cost approaches to distribution are described. Suffice it here to observe that in the marketing structures of the next decade, a rapprochement between the physical handling and distribution activity and channel strategy must take place, and that within this sector, routinization has a very substantial role indeed to play. Service level cost implications have already been described; transportation problems of vehicle scheduling and the like are all susceptible to logically more valid analytical solutions than we have traditionally been accustomed to implement in marketing. Despite such a growing concern with routinized logistics, however, the task of channel liaison can probably most sensibly remain linked with the personal sales activity sphere when a business is selling via intermediaries as well as directly. It is this sphere which already has the face-to-face contact. Our evidence in Part C shows that a little more than half of major British companies do use intermediaries, although this figure falls substantially for industrial and rises considerably for consumer goods manufacturers. (See Tables C.10, C.11 and C.12.)

Two other departments of operational marketing merit comment here. Promotional activity has linked, as a task, with presonal sales activity under the general umbrella of external, persuasive, communications. For two or more decades lip-service has been paid to the concept that personal sales activity and above-the-line promotions are substitutable in part, or even in whole, one for the other. Institutional structures have conspired, by placing a senior sales executive and a senior advertising man in direct contact with the chief marketing executive to prevent any critical or serious exploration of possible trade-offs between these two major alternative media for persuasive external communications. The task for the marketing activity in this field is clearly to identify and deploy the optimal media of communication in the optimum mix. The historically dominant and discrete status of sales and above-the-line advertising demands mitigation in the seventies and beyond, and this is a further problematic functional element in our current concepts of marketing organization. If such an external communications orientation can be developed strategically, at the routinized level of operational activity such co-ordination of implementation must be present.

A further element of such co-ordination must also emerge. It is the integrated consideration of above- and below-the-line promotional effort in a total approach to the use of impersonal media of persuasive communication. As our colleague, Martin Christopher, who has worked with a team of Bradford faculty members and senior executives from Horniblow, Cox-Freeman, the advertising agents, has demonstrated, such co-ordinated consideration seldom takes place. Within the operational marketing sphere, such co-ordination must be firmly integrated within the media planning and selection routines of the business.*

Our final area for concern must be the operational selection and management of marketing staff in a markedly more professional manner. The contributions of occupational psycholo-

---

* Martin Christopher's study, *Marketing Below the Line* is published by Allen and Unwin, in its Studies in Management Series, 1972. The studies on which it was based were funded by Horniblow, Cox-Freeman. A new 3-year study funded by upwards of a dozen business firms is just beginning at the Management Centre on the joint consideration of above- and below-the-line promotion and measurement of its effectiveness. Results are due in 1974.

142 ORGANIZATIONAL DESIGN FOR MARKETING FUTURES

gists to the identification of skills and attitudes which are correlated with sales success are better known than the very very small amount of work done to date on staffing policies in the logistics and communications fields. A considerable body of knowledge exists which enhances our understanding of those characteristics likely to yield success in new product development fields. The task of implementing this knowledge in terms of recruitment testing and the like lagged severely in the marketing climate of the sixties. This is explicable in terms of the style of approach which marketing had inherited from the sales-oriented era of British business, both before World War II and after the Korean War. Not only can extant knowledge be routinely administered; the emergent knowledge of the seventies should be more rapidly routinized than previously.

In parallel with the routinization of selection procedures, however, must come a coherent effort to improve operational marketing management in general. The application of profit centre approaches and management-by-objectives has long characterized operational marketing, most noticeably through the use of product and brand management systems of organization. Marketing is even notorious in many firms for the organic, flexible nature of its managerial approach – too casual and disrespectful are frequent descriptions by traditionalists either of the Theory X schools of thought or from more mechanistic or bureaucratic functions in the business. If all our comments about routinization of operational marketing activity mean anything, they mean a noticeable but not an irrevocable shift, away from the casual, organic, flexible approach in the management of current operations and the relegation of much but not all of that flair, hunch, brilliance and creativity which can only thrive in the organic flexible structure to that sector of the business concerned with Marketing Development.

It is to Marketing Development and its interface with Research and Development in the technical sector that we shall now turn our attention. As we do, however, it behoves us to make one comment concerning the observations we have just made on routinization of operational marketing activity and on the following seven sets of observations on the problems of marketing's organizational transfer to meet the tasks of the next decade. We have hypothesized the firms which we discuss in

ORGANIZATIONAL TRANSFER – ORGANIZATIONAL DEVELOPMENT 143

general terms to be relatively dependent on the development of new technology; we have hypothesized that they are concerned with the fields of basic research. We realize that not all firms will be so based or concerned. Hence our observations will seldom if ever be a neat fit for any particular firm, and we have not sought to make them so. Rather, we hope that the flow of ideas and their conceptualization will trigger thoughts in the mind of the reader which stimulate him or her to do the organizational-relating, to contemplate the organizational transfer problems from his contemporary corporate base with his contemporary and anticipated resources, both human and physical.

Neither are we suggesting that, because certain tasks have been identified here as 'marketing' tasks, they should be the exclusive preserve of the marketer with full corporate responsibility. All the empirical evidence we have collected shows that would be a naive conception and we do not wish to propose it. We have dashed and dotted certain boxes as obviously not marketing's preserve; we could have dotted more, since many tasks will be shared.

Finally, we are not suggesting that each task in every company should have a full-time employee to perform it. Many businesses will be able to combine some of these tasks in the recruitment job specification of one man. That is fine so long as the awareness and critical importance of these future tasks are perceived.

D.2. THE FUSION OF MARKETING DEVELOPMENT AND TECHNICAL RESEARCH AND DEVELOPMENT

It would be erroneous of us to suggest that routinization is solely a dimension of the operational marketing task. The activity of marketing development within the company requires a considerable degree of routinization as well. The formalized generation of new ideas, the conscious structuring of dynamic, organic, flexible structures which encourage the birth of new ideas and their gestation into products or services are each susceptible to routine without stultification. The procedures for screening and comparatively evaluating a vast reservoir of new ideas, product concepts and scenarios are routines. The

144   ORGANIZATIONAL DESIGN FOR MARKETING FUTURES

standardized panoply of marketing research techniques for new product testing or for simulation of alternative competitive strategies are further instances. And in each of these sectors the routinization process can be seen actively at work. Hence, in the sector of business activity concerned with marketing development we shall be less concerned with the issue of routinization than with a shift in the balance of the developmental activities of marketing. We see the prime requirement to be a fusion of Marketing Development activity with the technical work undertaken in what we generally know as R & D.

This will not be the only dimension of our developmental concern, but it is the one we see as most critical. Other vitally important shifts in emphasis have already been trailed in our consideration of operational marketing in Section D.1 above – the need for a total external communications approach at the strategic level and a concentration on strategy in the channel/logistics and funding areas of the business.

The lynchpin of the fusion we see as necessary is the process of technological forecasting (TF), allied in many instances to the emergent technology of social forecasting. A recent investigation amongst British industry* has indicated that TF has to date gained only a marginal foothold within the total planning process of the business within our most progressive concerns. Even in these companies, the scope of its implementation is sporadic and partial with only the simplest and most imaginative techniques, such as the Delphi forecast method, in use. The requirement to master technology or be mastered by it must, however, ensure a continued development of TF activity at both corporate and national levels – we say this despite the early steps at dismantling the Ministry of Technology's strategic activities which the Heath Government undertook in 1970 when the Ministry of Technology merged with the Board of Trade to form the Ministry for Trade and Industry.

Technological forecasting brings, perforce, the technical planner and the marketing development activity together; the one to plan a technical capability and the other to assess the market availability for any such capacity when it may reach fruition. The divorce of these two processes, the tendency to

* Currill, D., M.Sc. dissertation presented in the University of Bradford Management Centre, September 1970.

ORGANIZATIONAL TRANSFER – ORGANIZATIONAL DEVELOPMENT 145

bring the marketer in only as an afterthought once any given technological capability has emerged, has been a costly phenomenon for British companies for decades and virtually catastrophic for the British economy. We only have to look at Japanese technology in the fifties and sixties to see clearly what can be achieved by the intelligent fusion of marketing and technical development. The marketing development function of the seventies has to combat, simultaneously, both technological and marketing myopia, and TF is the arena in which that combat is forced and, hopefully, resolved. Our enthusiasm for TF should not be thought to advance the case that it is a panacea for development problems. It is, rather, an aid to minimize the difficulties and to clarify the objectives of corporate techno/ market strategy. Nor can the marketing development expert be expected to prepare technological forecasts. He will not have the technical expertise. What the marketing activity can contribute, and where the marketing task lies, is the probabilistic assessment of the time dimension of market availability. It is worth noting, if fairly apparent, that a technical development programme which brings a new project to fruition a year or so too late for the market is often a severe handicap in competitive terms. A less apparent danger is the premature commitment of R & D resources and the incurrence of marketing investment as well, before the flow of market derived revenue can sensibly justify it. A completed product development which is a year or so ahead of market availability is capital fruitlessly tied up, and the implications of a too early completion of technology must be simultaneously considered with the costs of delay. This type of cost is frequently encountered in the component technologies which go to make up an aggregated delivered technological capability. The slack time which the conscious building in of delays into development programmes can generate is normally seen as a method of allocating resources to other more critical tasks. Such a concept is implicit in most of the CPA and PERT techniques of network analysis and indeed in Normative Relevance Tree Analysis in TF. Slack time may, however, be something we seek to generate quite specifically as a way of slowing down the movement forward of component capabilities ahead of the critical need for their completion, especially if sizeable financial or human resource commitments are involved.

K

146 ORGANIZATIONAL DESIGN FOR MARKETING FUTURES

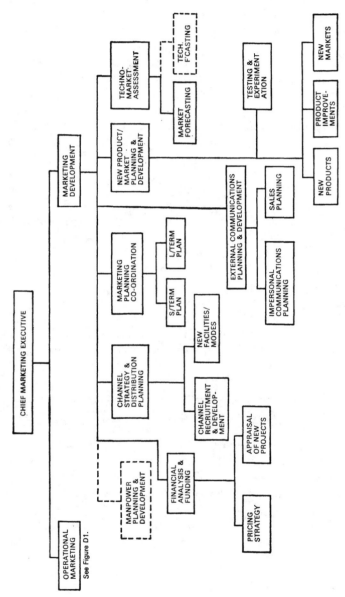

Figure D.2 MARKETING DEVELOPMENT'S ORGANIZATIONAL TASKS

ORGANIZATIONAL TRANSFER – ORGANIZATIONAL DEVELOPMENT 147

Figure D.2 indicates the preference we have for hypothesizing that the task of TF should be partly encompassed within the over-all activity of techno-market assessment under the aegis of the marketing development activity. Two separate sectors would prepare the detailed technological and market forecasts which would provide the assessable information. This assessment function would be separated conceptually from the more tradi-tional new product/market planning and development task of the firm, although there would undoubtedly be considerable cross communication between the two areas especially if they were operated within the company by different groups. It will be commonplace, for example, for market-derived new product ideas to be fed into the techno-market assessment activity via the new product/market planning route.

Within the new product/market planning and development task, the formal routinized techniques for the development of new ideas will be appropriate as alluded to earlier on. In par-ticular the specific consideration of each of the product/market sectors identified in Ansoff's now famous matrix for growth must be encompassed. These are typically as shown in Table D.1, with each of eight possible positions demanding change and development in one form or another. It is obvious that some

TABLE D.1 *Product/Market Planning and Development Dimensions*

		TECHNOLOGY BASE		
		EXISTING	IMPROVED	NEW
M A R K E T	EXISTING	NO CHANGE	PRODUCT IMPROVEMENT	PRODUCT DEVELOPMENT
B A S E	EXTENDED	MARKET EXTENSION		
	NEW	MARKET DEVELOPMENT		DIVERSIFICATION

148 ORGANIZATIONAL DESIGN FOR MARKETING FUTURES

make greater demands on TF, and others on the market forecasting arms of the techno/market assessment task.

We have already mentioned in our discussion of operational marketing that the promotional elements of marketing activity are likely to require a substantial restructuring during the decade ahead. It must be within Marketing Development that plans for this are laid. A useful dichotomy may well be between the deployment of human resources in face-to-face contact and the use of impersonal methods of persuasive communication both above- and below-the-line. The strategic alternatives must be evaluated and the total and marginal benefits of resource allocation in given directions assessed, as well as maintained under continuous review. Such a fundamental examination of strategy must also be undertaken within the field of channels of distribution and modes for the physical movement of goods and raw materials. This, as has been indicated, is an area of vast potential development in the seventies and beyond and will be given specific, discrete consideration in Section D.5 below.

Marketing's interplay with the financial area of the business in the strategic analysis of growth opportunities in its turn must undergo some considerable development. Two major fields of interaction are apparent – the development of a pricing strategy and the appraisal of new projects as they come forward. This latter task will of course be undertaken in alliance with the technical evaluation of new product concepts and the various stages of market assessment already described. For today's marketers to make any really coherent contribution in this sector of the company's marketing development, however, will require an extensive programme of education and training in the field of finance. The objectives of such training will not be to make finance experts out of marketers but rather intelligent colleagues in the co-ordinated planning process.

The fulcrum of all these separate tasks in marketing development is that major area of concern which we have left for comment until last – Marketing Planning Co-ordination. This is marketing's answer to the corporate planning backlash as manifest in so many business organizations at the turn of this decade. Through such an institutionalized task, the senior marketing development officer can ensure that his chief marketing executive is participating fully in the pattern of planning for the

ORGANIZATIONAL TRANSFER – ORGANIZATIONAL DEVELOPMENT 149

company's future whilst avoiding a technologically myopic view. In addition, equally difficult areas such as financial management are encompassed providing a more efficient grass roots approach towards planning than the present top-downwards-push which characterizes extant corporate planning methodology. A typical advantage of a grass roots development of marketing planning is the greater attention paid to the marketing strengths of the company. Symbiotic marketing and synergetic marketing, building perhaps on an extensive branding investment or on existing channels of distribution, tend to be more carefully and systematically attended to than under top-downwards-push planning.

Once again, we would enter a caveat. The Marketing Development task is not to overthrow or oust the corporate planning activity of the business. It is to cogently reassert marketing's involvement, as a sensibly reformed corporate animal, in the total planning process of the business. By the intelligent development of well co-ordinated and compatible plans, compatible that is with technological capability and funding possibilities, such a role can surely be re-established.

D.3. THE CUSTOMER SERVICE FUNCTION

Marketing research emerged as a body of viable, objective research techniques in the twenties and thirties of this century when mass markets had led to a breakdown of personal acquaintance with customers. The media of communications such as press and posters have much earlier origins in the fifteenth and sixteenth centuries. Yet to this day the procedures for customers to communicate spontaneously with manufacturer or producer have not existed. The signs are, however, present that 'consumerism', as it has been dubbed, will play an increasingly important part in the scrutiny of marketing activity in Britain. It accordingly behoves the manufacturer to explore the ways in which consumerism and the problems which gave rise to its growth, can be harnessed for corporate as well as social benefit.

The issue which we wish to examine in this section, under the heading of the customer service function of the business concerns the flow of service activities and information *within* the

150   ORGANIZATIONAL DESIGN FOR MARKETING FUTURES

company's field of present custom. Hence, market research techniques, as we conventionally know them, are not directly relevant to the task. The analogy can usefully be drawn with the internal pattern of company communications. We wish to focus attention most especially on the return flow of information and particularly complaints or criticisms from customers.

It is a well-known statistic, although the costing methods used are shrouded in mystery, that the direct cost of returning a defective component from a customer to producer is *nine times greater* than that of sending it out in the first instance. There can be little doubt that the factor by which return costs exceed outward flow costs is similar in many fields of marketing activity provided always that we look at the direct cost only. We must not lose sight of the fact, however, that there may be a considerable number of other costs to the company which will not be incurred if a defect is put right. Future business, for instance, may be held or new business secured.

It is our belief that the marketing activity in the seventies must build into its operational workings a formalized and carefully monitored customer service activity which we have termed a filter. Its possible location is indicated in Figure D.3. To this filter we would direct all feedback received from customers of whatever nature – directly by mail or phone, or obliquely from the personal sales activity, technical advisory staff, legal authorities or consumer organizations. It would be the task of this customer service filtration unit to ensure that a correct valuation of the views and complaints is made and that, wherever necessary, the competent operational executives or marketing development planners are made aware of a situation.

The corporate ombudsman function is seemingly inescapable as the complexities of customer contact increase and an escalating range of specialist intermediaries intervene to distort effective communication, and as the competitive importance of securing and retaining happy, satisfied customers grows.

Figure D.3 specifically differentiates between institutional and individual customers because their relationships and potency of communication backwards to a manufacturer will vary widely. However, the situations are perhaps more similar than we often realize. Precisely the same factors as those which have given rise to the particular growth of consumerism have led to

Organizational Transfer – Organizational Development 151

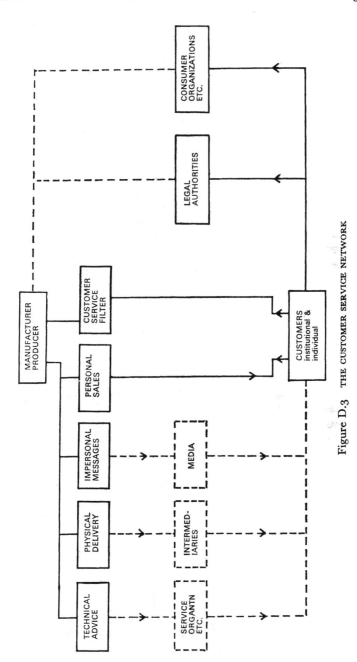

Figure D.3   THE CUSTOMER SERVICE NETWORK

152   ORGANIZATIONAL DESIGN FOR MARKETING FUTURES

the enhanced professionalization of the industrial purchasing function in British industry and to the concept of countervailing power in the retail and wholesale trades most typically seen with Marks and Spencer and the supermarketing multiple chains. In each of these instances, the professional has spoken up to make himself felt in default of the effective working of the customer sovereignty concept of marketing folklore. Whereas the business can easily take the initiative to establish a customer service filtration unit, the implications for dealing with countervailing power from either the professional industrial purchasing function or the large channel member are less clear. Pragmatic approaches have predominated with working formulae about the proportion of total revenue which can safely be accorded to any large customers. A more coherent approach is demanded in the seventies. A segmented within-company consideration of customers is the obvious first step, along power lines rather than product dimensions. Lessons learnt, for example, in terms of client management within the advertising agency world can usefully be transferred to help cope with the situation. Although the problem is in absolute terms insoluble, much of the risk and uncertainty can be taken out as effective customer liaison is built up with major, sophisticated buyers. Not only can the remainder of the producer organization benefit from what it learns from its more sophisticated customers. The customers themselves can come to depend on a wide range of ancillary advice and service from the producer which makes a change of supplier a costly step to consider.

In both its dimensions, with institutional and individual customers, the demands of the customer service function in the seventies can only be met effectively by a positive awareness of the problems posed and the need to face up to them in a structured way.

D.4.   MARKETING INTELLIGENCE SYSTEMS

Marketing research techniques have traditionally been used for the *ad hoc*, static analysis of marketing problems. Although in the field of fast-moving consumer goods such as groceries and pharmaceuticals such techniques as the retail audit and the consumer panel have given more potential for dynamism, these sectors have been uncharacteristic of the great majority of organizations. Marketing research has not generally speaking been employed to monitor the marketing environment on a continuing basis. However, a major shift in orientation within previously largely *ad hoc* users of marketing research, and the conversion of new organizations and service industries to the use of such techniques, has led to a considerable change in organizational requirements. This movement, involving a transformation of task, demands our reconsideration of organizational design in the seventies. We have already identified the need for marketing data in the planning and co-ordinating role which we have hypothesized within the area of marketing development and indicated the need for short-term market measurement data to guide operational marketing activities. The total process can usefully be conceptualized in an overall view of the marketing process within society and the role for a marketing intelligence system within it.

The total systems approach to marketing information is posited on a thorough analysis of intelligence requirements for the individual organization under study. Any normative statement of information needs must necessarily be arbitrary, but there can be no doubt that if it is to be increasingly effective as a starting point for systems design then the senior intelligence officer must necessarily be privy to the formulation of future directions for development by the business. Too frequently in the past decade the information function has failed to meet corporate intelligence needs due to insufficient warning of an impending demand such as that occasioned by a policy of market extension overseas or product line extension in the domestic market.

We have no wish to enter a plea that the information function in the business should necessarily have the answer to all marketing demands made upon it for the most unlikely information. Adequate cost–benefit analysis can show the general level at which information can be expected to be held. This does, however, require a careful analysis of the cost of bringing in information from outside the corporate system and the implications to the company profit situation of any delays. It also demands a rigorous examination of the value of information to the business organization. Our work during the past five years

154 ORGANIZATIONAL DESIGN FOR MARKETING FUTURES

on test marketing and experimental method in British industry has shown us that a logical use is not always made of empirical research findings and that action is often taken prior to the arrival of data which have been commissioned at considerable expense.*

This is not the place to develop in any detail how the cost–benefit analysis of marketing information can be accomplished. We have indicated some theoretical approaches elsewhere. Nonetheless, it is a field of activity which will demand great effort at refinement in the seventies if the problem of arriving at sensible intelligence budgets is to be grappled and coped with.

Slater, a recent research associate at the University of Bradford, has suggested a simplified model of the information and decision flows in a typical corporate marketing intelligence system.† It is shown at Figure D.4.

One of the most significant transformations of information organization implicit in the systems approach is the conceptual integration of internally derived data and both styles of the externally derived – either specifically commissioned investigation reports or general data available to all in a competitive framework. The concept of a central information unit or data bank is then implicitly grafted into the integrated data processing system of the fifties and sixties which carries out conventional analyses of customer accounts and sales, giving budget variances etcetera.

The opportunity for interrogation of the information unit or data bank also arises and constitutes one of the most important additional strengths of marketing in the corporate power structure as it moves into the seventies. The models, the construction of which the creation of a data bank facilitates, will enable extensive simulation of marketing alternatives in planning future strategies as well as the accomplishment of sensitive response to short-term vicissitudes in the operational marketing sector of affairs.

The response function of the market is, after all, the great unknown in business. The simulation potential will increasingly

* This work which deals with the whole spectrum of test marketing activity is to be published later in Allen and Unwin's Studies in Management Series under the title *Test Marketing*, by Roy Hayhurst.

† Alan Slater's report, *The Organizational Structure for Marketing Information*, was presented for his M.Sc. degree in September, 1970 at the University of Bradford Management Centre. Copies are available.

ORGANIZATIONAL TRANSFER – ORGANIZATIONAL DEVELOPMENT 155

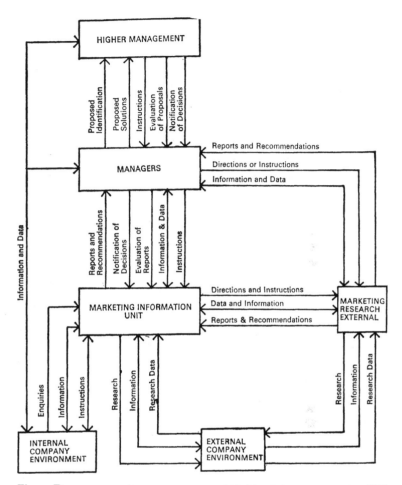

Figure D.4 MODEL OF INFORMATION AND DECISION FLOWS FOR A MARKETING INTELLIGENCE SYSTEM (after Slater)

afford the opportunity to reduce the gross level of uncertainty under which any business operates, although we would be the last to suggest it will remove the need for creative judgement in the context of simulation outputs.

The advantages of the central computerized holding of marketing information seem to us to outweigh the benefits which can be obtained by each division or product level of marketin

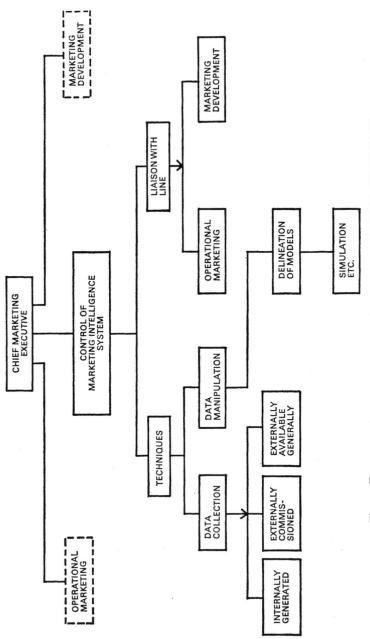

Figure D.5 STRUCTURE OF TYPICAL MARKETING INTELLIGENCE SYSTEM TASKS

ORGANIZATIONAL TRANSFER – ORGANIZATIONAL DEVELOPMENT 157

activity maintaining its own monitoring procedures. Hence, our postulated organizational framework isolates the marketing intelligence system from every main line activity and proffers a staff service with a strong line liaison activity in operation. In particular, the liaison staff need to be men or women who comprehend the full scope of the marketing activity and see the research and data facility they provide as the servant of the line activity. This staffing requirement demands a new breed of specialist of whom we shall have more to say later on in Section D.8. Within the data bank core of the intelligence system activity, the specialist statisticians, mathematicians and computer experts are to be found. Figure D.5 indicates a typical organization which we envisage.

The starting point for this type of structure is, of course, the operational or development executive within the organization. It is their requirements which the intelligence system must meet and they both, through their chief marketing executive and through their own senior colleagues, must ensure that the intelligence objectives are clearly established and reviewed. Granted these premises, the cogency with which marketing activities can be directed in the decade before us will be grandly enhanced.

D.5. TOTAL DISTRIBUTION APPROACHES

We have referred, on a considerable number of occasions already, to the advent of new thinking about logistics and the physical movement of goods and raw materials from their origins to their point of ultimate consumption. The revolution which has taken place conceptually in this area during the sixties must be translated into operational practice. In essence, the physical distribution management, or PDM concept as it has been called, involves undermining one facet of conventional marketing mix thinking. The PDM concept posits that the selection of channels for distribution and the physical arrangements for movement can be most effectively seen as a co-ordinated area of cost concern. Such an approach also brings together the formerly discrete areas of activity which we know as warehousing, despatch and transportation as well as the critical field of stock control procedures. Figure D.6 indicates the co-

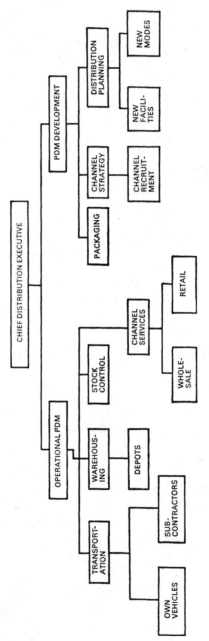

Figure D.6 THE CO-ORDINATED PATTERN OF PHYSICAL DISTRIBUTION MANAGEMENT

ORGANIZATIONAL TRANSFER – ORGANIZATIONAL DEVELOPMENT 159

ordinated pattern of tasks towards which many organizations are now moving.

In Figure D.6 we have shown a chief distribution executive heading up the co-ordinating role. In any business with a substantial element of distribution expenditure, for instance, sugar, oil, and other bulky low-value products, this role will almost certainly be exercised full time. In other businesses with a less substantial concern for distribution the co-ordinative task may well be exercised by the chief marketing executive. The nominal head's designation notwithstanding, the principle of trade-offs between one sector of distribution activity and another must not be lost. It is this co-ordination payoff which has hitherto been missed by businesses and which promises very substantial improvements in effectiveness in the not-too-distant future for firms which adopt the total cost approach to their PDM.

The principle of cost trade-offs between, for instance, transportation and stock holding, or depot location, can only be fully operationally effective if adequate cost data are to hand. Currently this is not generally the case and it points to an urgent need in the seventies for considerable development in costing procedures.

The most obvious examples of trade-offs have been furnished in recent years by the use of air freight – the most expensive mode of transportation available but one which can frequently be justified. In terms of small-weight, high-value items air freighting enables minimal centralized stocks to be held for immediate transportation on demand. The high cost of transportation is offset by the reduced cost of stock holding not just in terms of the absolute number of units necessary to guarantee a given service level, but also in terms of the overhead costs of warehouse or depot management, insurance, etcetera.

The PDM expert, of whom there are precious few at the present time, seeks the minimum total distribution cost for a delivered level of service. It is this qualification to minimum total cost which places marketing firmly in touch with the PDM activity. What is the optimum level of service? Certainly it will very seldom be one hundred per cent availability at twenty-four hours' notice. The cost of such a service level, albeit presently imprecisely measured, is infinitely greater than 66 per cent service at five days' notice. The cost implications of the

160 ORGANIZATIONAL DESIGN FOR MARKETING FUTURES

alternative levels of service must be explored and the value of service levels in gaining and retaining customers assessed.

One early and logical conclusion frequently derived from such an approach is the development of a differential treatment of customers in the service level context. A level of service is afforded which is compatible with the value of the customer's patronage to the firm.

The obverse of a total distribution cost approach is, of course, currently widely practised. It involves cost minimization in each area, for example in transportation or stock holding costs. Well, the cheapest transportation system is undoubtedly that where the customer collects his product when he orders it; and the cheapest stock-holding policy is no stocks at all. But these courses of action are seldom likely to optimize the corporate profitability contribution from the distribution sector.

Two issues which are familiar marketing territory are highlighted in a total approach to PDM. The first is packaging. The PDM development area of concern needs to think long and hard about packaging – not in its aesthetic sense but in terms of its functional contribution to the improvement of physical distribution effectiveness. Key concern is with the protective aspects of packages and outers but also with the absolute size of these two packs as well.

Channel strategy is hitherto familiar marketing territory as well, along with the task of channel member recruitment. Whilst it is seldom open to producers to switch from one channel to the next at very short notice, the critical need to keep the channels through which products are being distributed under review cannot be over-emphasized. In recent years many markets have slipped from one pattern of distribution to another with many producers caught unaware. New diversification possibilities also present themselves, such as the use of mail order or going direct to the end customer in addition to conventional approaches.

However, a new market initiative frequently provides the opportunity to try a new, more hopeful approach to distribution channels, especially in overseas markets. There is seldom any good reason to duplicate home patterns of activity without a careful evaluation of all the alternatives. Channels should be

ORGANIZATIONAL TRANSFER – ORGANIZATIONAL DEVELOPMENT 161

chosen as carefully as media for impersonal communications are selected; but they hardly ever are.

Equally, a thorough analysis of new modes of transportation, such as containerization should be continually maintained within the PDM development sector alongside the more conventional task of inaugurating new facilities.

Having attempted here to extend the marketing horizon to include a comprehension and concern for total PDM, we would be unwise to close these comments without a short comment on the logistics function in general. A business' goods and materials do not only flow outwards from the business; they flow inwards and around the firm as they are processed. Although these two additional activities covering the physical movement of goods and materials are traditionally taken care of by procurement or purchasing departments and by materials management expertise within the production activity, scope sometimes exists for a wider application of trade-off analysis. Goods as materials inwards may be providing an empty load back to whence they came which is of benefit to the PDM function in the firm. The delivery times and points for raw materials and their handling may equally be programmed to the improvement of corporate activity. Contract purchasing and delivery have begun to improve results in this area.

Our caveat, therefore, to the too introverted adoption of an exclusively marketing logistics approach is that other trade-offs may exist for corporate benefit and it behoves us to examine the total logistics function of the firm at the outset.

D.6. THE INTERNATIONAL DIMENSION

Our specific empirical investigation of marketing organization structures reported in Part C, did not encompass the international aspects of the business. This was a field about which relatively more was known at the time we commenced our study. Hence, our hypothesized pattern for organizational transfer must be based on our reading of the evidence collected by others. Fortunately, it seems reasonably clear that firms begin to export as an escape from problems in their domestic market. They normally begin with the appointment of one agent or so. If business prospers, they will frequently progress

L

thereafter to a locally based overseas selling organization and thence to a semi-autonomous manufacturing capacity. Many national policies, especially in the developing countries, have accelerated this trend in recent years by providing tax incentives and tariff disincentives to skip the early stages. Each step is, however, a critical stage in the overall learning process through which a firm goes about new markets. Exporting on this casual learning sequence is a distinctly different phenomenon from the concept of the international business which is increasingly dominating the pattern of world trading relations. The old theoretical explanations of trade arising from a comparative cost advantage between one economic system and the next is superfluous in the face of the giant investing companies who seek a return on the assets they have at their disposal and remit in money terms to their investing public.

Whereas a familiar export structure for marketing will either presently include a full range of product managers in the domestic company with international as well as domestic responsibility, or executives with a total international concern, the future pattern looks distinctly different. Virtually the only element within the parent business which will have any direct line concern with overseas operations is the financial division. It is the company's financial experts who occupy themselves

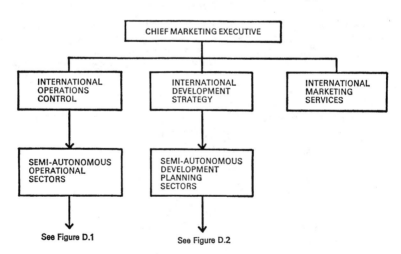

Figure D.7 THE INTERNATIONAL DIMENSION TO THE MARKETING TASK

ORGANIZATIONAL TRANSFER – ORGANIZATIONAL DEVELOPMENT 163

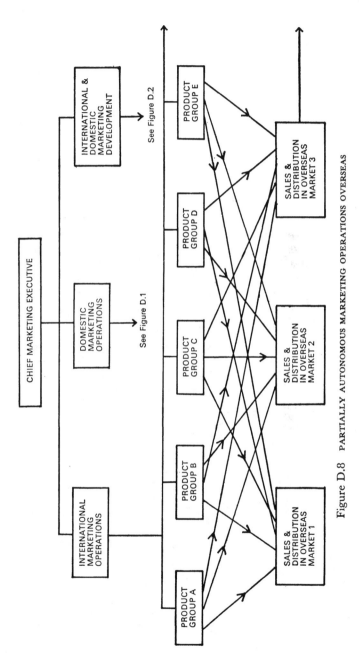

Figure D.8 PARTIALLY AUTONOMOUS MARKETING OPERATIONS OVERSEAS

164   ORGANIZATIONAL DESIGN FOR MARKETING FUTURES

with setting target rates of return on assets employed overseas and with ensuring that they are met. The parent company's marketing activity may have only a residual staff or advisory role for overseas markets and a co-ordinating strategic role; but this latter is better undertaken by a holding company, rather than an operational parent from a single economic culture.

Within each viable economic market overseas – be it clustered countries or nation state – a marketing activity analogous to that which we have postulated in D.1 through D.5 can sensibly exist. At the holding company focus, a simple organizational pattern as shown in Figure D.7 may well suffice.

The advantages of allowing each viable economic market region to proceed as autonomously as possible are well rehearsed. Most importantly, the cultural differences between different markets can be adequately taken into account. Additionally, however, the problems posed by centralized control in terms of sclerotic channels of communication and the stultification of initiative can most effectively be conquered.

Nonetheless, there are and will continue to be situations in which the operational aspects only of marketing activity are passed over to semi-autonomous organizations within the overseas marketing sectors. The task of marketing development is then considerably complicated since decisions must be taken at a distance and plans passed on to operational executives some considerable distance away. This latter course of action almost invariably requires the employment of expatriate executives who are familiar with the back-home planning and development processes. Figure D.8 indicates a pattern of organization which has begun to emerge and which may well prove a valuable blueprint for an increasing number of businesses en route to the virtually autonomous divisions of an international business.

D.7. ETHICS AND AESTHETICS

Marketing ethics are not something which can be left to the legal department to guard over. An emphasis on an ethical approach has to permeate each and every decision-making point within the organization. (Most marketers can easily agree with these two opening statements.) The key starting point for any such permeation, however, must be an overt

ORGANIZATIONAL TRANSFER – ORGANIZATIONAL DEVELOPMENT 165

statement of what is and is not deemed ethical at any point in time by the business. We deliberately say at any point in time because ethics in a society undergo a process of change and adjustment through time and it is incumbent on the marketeer to be sensitive to such changes. Such sensitivity is an integral part of the marketing development activity of the firm. Sometimes legal constraints may well run ahead, or lag behind, what seems to be the prevalent social view of ethical standards. Both these eventualities demand careful attention, and whilst the former can normally be expected to come forcibly to one's notice via professional associations and the like, the latter constitutes a continuous hazard.

The critical areas for ethical concern undoubtedly lie in product formulation and communications, and both these areas have been exhaustively reviewed in many corporate structures for several decades. Most obviously the instances of thalidomide and cyclamates come to mind, but cigarettes and birth control pills are of a similar ilk.

We believe that in many firms formal ethical analysis of product formulation is not undertaken, and that in the communications sector it is almost invariably left to the agents concerned with below- or above-the-line activity. In the personal sales activity, greater involvement exists but is not always recognized as a critical area for attention. At a social level, the arguments in favour of adopting an ethical approach can be taken as given; at a commercial level there is often detailed debate as to whether it is better to err or not from the conventional social norms. No total answer can be furnished of course except to say that doubtful behaviour by customers or requests by them for gifts or bribes can seldom pay in the medium or long term. Where the dividing line between the demands for additional preferred discounts by large channel members, for instance, and straight bribery from smaller firms comes, is a moot point. Organizationally, we advance the argument that the firm must face up to these issues. It can usefully have a policy document on the subject which is given to all levels within the corporate structure and to which employees are required to adhere. Putting an ethical code down on paper is a hazardous and a heart-searching process; it is one which companies must face up to in the seventies. It will become increasingly

166 ORGANIZATIONAL DESIGN FOR MARKETING FUTURES

indispensable to successful trading, both with the trade and with final consumers.

Such a document can be expected to be partially concerned with the pattern of future development of product offerings. It may well complement a separate functional activity of testing such as has been devised in the pharmaceutical and food industries. Its strategic importance is that it makes the company take a conscious approach to ethical issues and thereby reduces the chances that contemporary standards or legal requirements can be sinned against. It logically fits within the domain of the customer service function of the business and if the earlier hypothesized liaison unit is incorporated within a company's marketing organization structure, ethical documentation and scrutiny can legitimately be written into its task definition.

Where the law affords no guidelines or coercion, ethical standards are open to argument; the field of aesthetics offers even more scope for dissent. There can be little doubt, however, that both in the field of consumer goods packaging and product design a great deal more concern must be shown by marketing in the seventies. Hitherto, the general pattern of organization has been to employ design consultants for packaging tasks and to leave the product design aspects predominantly in the hands of the engineers and draughtsmen. A number of organizations have shown a way forward to a total integrated concern for the design and aesthetic activities of the company as a whole. This is perhaps most characteristic of the communications sector with integrated house styles and the accelerating use of symbols, but only in a few instances has it been extended to a totally compatible product design concept – Marks and Spencer or Habitat are perhaps good examples in the producer-to-retailer business.

We can hypothesize that within organizations which place a considerable reliance on design in an aesthetic sense as well as those concerned predominantly with functionality, a considerably enhanced role for the design activity will necessarily materialize and that this is a socially desirable trend which will enhance the quality of life. Innovative organization structuring in this respect can accordingly expect to provide considerable payoffs. We see the role for a design activity, concerned with aesthetics and functionality, as paralleling the recent rapid

ORGANIZATIONAL TRANSFER – ORGANIZATIONAL DEVELOPMENT 167

development of value analysis and engineering. Design in its aesthetic dimension will be increasingly 'valued' in a product or service offering, be it an industrial product or a piece of bank or insurance documentation. The value analysis activity of the firm must take this into account.

A design activity within the organization will reside between the production and the marketing sectors as it manifests concern especially in functionality and appearance. In both instances it will be predominantly involved in the planning and development aspects, but it will, of course, utilize present operational feedback as well as pure creativity in its work.

In summary, we would comment that value analysis and value engineering require a wider concept of the value to be analysed in functional terms, to embrace the aesthetic dimension. This we feel can best be accomplished by a Design Unit within the business with a creative and watching brief, whenever design is an integral contributor to marketing efficacy.

D.8. EDUCATIONAL DEVELOPMENT AND TRAINING

In the education and training area of marketing's task there are two separate goals to be attained. The first, and the one which has hitherto mesmerized much of marketing's involvement during the sixties, is training in the techniques of current best practice. Although there is widespread evidence that many chief marketing executives have attended courses of one type or another, there is a general atmosphere of under-development of practical expertise. Rigorous utilization of marketing research procedures, stringent attempts to assess optimum ways of deploying promotional budgets and the like, are far from universally present although most chief marketing executives are in agreement that these tasks must be carried out within their organizations.

There can be no escape, in the seventies and beyond, from the critical need to structure into the marketing organization a formalized pattern of analysis of training requirements to meet effectively the operational marketing tasks. This we have hypothesized in Figure D.1 as a Staffing and Personnel Management requirement. In Figure D.9 this task is related to the

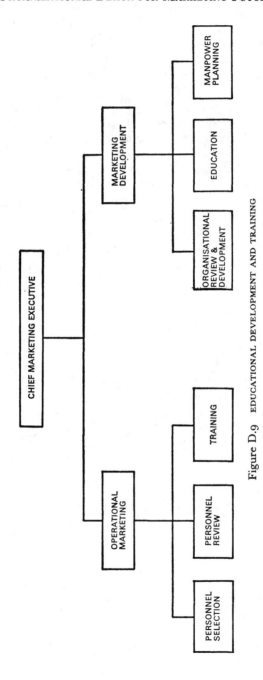

Figure D.9   EDUCATIONAL DEVELOPMENT AND TRAINING

ORGANIZATIONAL TRANSFER – ORGANIZATIONAL DEVELOPMENT 169

allied task within Marketing Development which involves Manpower Planning and Development.

Whether, in any particular firm, these tasks are done under line authority from the chief marketing executive, or on a staff basis by a personnel activity for the whole organization, is an issue which will depend on the circumstances. What must be accomplished in the decade ahead is a ready awareness of the need for line marketing executives to be involved at both the operational and the development levels of activity.

Personnel selection procedures are increasingly applied at a formal level to sales staff, but very little attempt has been made to work more widely within the marketing area. Only a few limited experiments have been made in marketing research staff selection.

Equally, the concept of training, both on an in-company basis and via external courses, must be embraced and formally implemented in the operational sector of the business beyond the sales area. There is a noticeable need for such training in public relations and below-the-line promotion as well as in the above-the-line advertising sector. The most urgent need, however, is in the field of marketing logistics, both in terms of training in the scientific approaches of PDM and in the training of distribution channel members.

In the area of marketing development, the task requirements have been virtually untouched hitherto. What we have attempted to do in this book, at a macro level for UK marketing activity, is a constant requirement at the micro or individual firm level from hereon out. The preparation of scenarios of marketing futures and the planning and development of organization structures which will adequately meet those scenarios, is an urgent task. It will not require a rigid planning and development activity since the scenarios can never be more than probabilistic statements about the future, but once again a conscious effort is required. Each organization must do what we would encourage our reader here to do in the context of Part A – it must prepare its own scenarios and develop its own educational efforts to ensure that such scenarios can be effectively met if they finally eventuate.

Education of the existing staff members alone, however, cannot suffice. The total manpower requirements in numerical and qualitative terms must be assessed against the scenarios we write. This too involves a careful analysis in considerable detail of the overall pattern of marketing development envisaged. It will go a long way towards minimizing or even avoiding dire educational shortfalls such as those from which British marketing has had to suffer during the post-war decades. These have been, firstly, a chronic shortage of general marketing expertise which is still with us as we write and secondly, the looming shortfall in effective personnel for the logistics and PDM revolutions in company activities.

A third shortfall sector, for which a limited leadtime still exists, is the total communications approach to company external promotion activity at the personal and impersonal levels. In this field almost no educational provision is currently made, and no major business school or university institution has yet taken any meaningful steps in this direction. Nonetheless we must ensure the availability of a cadre of well-educated executives in this area for future British industry and for the advertising/communications agency world.

At the risk of seeming to enter a special plea for the educational sector in which we authors work, it is important to emphasize the minimal level of involvement of the highest education sector in marketing education. Not more than thirty Ph.D. students are currently at work in the field; there are barely 200 students following full courses in marketing at Masters degree level each year; there are still only a limited number of Chairs of Marketing in British Universities (Bradford, Lancaster, London Business School (2), Manchester Business School (2), Strathclyde, UMIST and Warwick, plus one in Agricultural Marketing at Newcastle and one in Horticultural Marketing at Wye College, London University). Several of these Chairs are predominantly research appointments or concerned with marketing research methodology, and the Chairs in the agricultural/horticultural sector probably have greater research resources than all other Chairs put together. British industry cannot assume that the higher education needs of marketing have now been taken care of, since a four or fivefold increase in provision can be clearly seen as necessary if the majority of our hypothesized futures materialize and they are to be met effectively.

The PDM sector view is somewhat clouded by the long-standing provision in the operational research and management science areas of some of the analytical skills required. Nonetheless, a very substantial shortfall in skilled provision exists in all quantitative sectors and the total PDM concept is seldom the basis for distribution analysis in the OR and management science schools in any event.

In the communications sector, a major initiative from the communications industries – both social and technological, the electronics manufacturers and the advertising agencies – is urgently necessary at once to prime the higher education sectors for the emergence and development of a thoroughly educated, competent, communicator for the topmost managerial tasks in the marketing activity.

None of these comments are intended to be in any way churlish about the support which many organizations are currently giving to higher education institutions to collate, codify and extend the body of knowledge and to disseminate that knowledge. Nor is any slight intended on the escalating involvement of the Polytechnic sector through CNAA degree courses in the education and training of marketing men and women. We are concerned with the present under-provision for, and under-realization of, the need for development at the frontiers of our knowledge in marketing. If forecasting means anything to us, and it is the marketing activity which has played such an important part in its corporate development, we must apply it to our educational sector as we expect companies to apply it to their sales and production activities.

D.9. THE PRESENT/FUTURE DICHOTOMY IN ORGANIZATIONAL DESIGN

It has been suggested by many to whom we have described our Marketing Operational/Marketing Development split in marketing tasks, that we were merely creating a new, unfamiliar problem of integration, in order to overcome a lesser problem – that of persuading marketing executives to spend somewhat more time thinking about the future in the course of an already integrated activity. In a small or small-medium firm we must partially accept such an argument and partially also concede that separation of the task in terms of specific individuals will not be economically feasible. Having made such a concession, we adhere firmly to our view that the two tasks demand formalized, separable treatment in the medium or large organization if they are to be effectively executed. Not only the future will benefit; the present pattern of operational activity will benefit also from its specific professionalization.

We already see the dichotomy between R & D and Production, and we see it emerging within the financial area of the business between straightforward budgetary control methods and the funding and financial appraisal tasks which are increasingly important.

We suggest that the venture group concept, so effectively employed now in many major corporations for new product development work, be conceptually extended to cover a much wider gamut of the marketing activity. Hence, we proposed that a continual movement of executive personnel in the marketing sector from the marketing development task to operational marketing, and then back to development, should be attempted. Obviously not all staff will be involved in this systematic movement. Specialists in forecasting activity and the like will remain in the development sector indefinitely, but plans will be operationally implemented by those executives who develop them. Such is the present pattern of activity, but the sabbatical concept of removing the operational executive from the operational sector for a full plan period to develop his next operational plan is not generally practised.

Such a rotation of key staff has two major advantages. Firstly, the planning is undertaken by men who have an intimate knowledge of the market in which operations will take place.

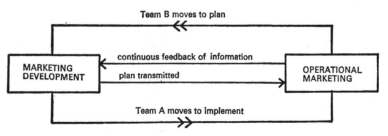

Figure D.10 PLANNING AND HUMAN RESOURCE MARKETING SYSTEM

Organizational Transfer – Organizational Development 173

Secondly, the implementation of plans will be in the hands of those who have devised them and had the opportunity to ensure that they are well laid. The cycle of planning and human rotation would be as indicated in Figure D.10 for two executive teams, A and B. The overall structure of tasks is indicated in Figure D.11.This integrates the thinking implicit in Figures D.1 and D.2. Such a pattern would need to be adapted if an international dimension, as posited in Figure D.8, is envisaged, but can stand unscathed if a virtually autonomous international business scheme is preferred.

One final caveat: we have no illusions that all these tasks will be the sole concern of the chief marketing executive. No man could co-ordinate them all alone. Many will be shared responsibilities with the other areas of activity in the firm. But, we hypothesize that they must be areas of marketing concern with some element of responsibility resting with the Chief Marketing Executive of the future.

We have had a single purpose in this endeavour. We have been anxious to indicate, not one hundred per cent certain scenarios, but a style of thinking both about marketing's future tasks, and about the way any particular marketing organization can arrange itself to meet the opportunities implicit in its future. We hope that our reader will feel it worthwhile to turn now to the organization with which he is familiar and apply the conceptual approach we have explored here.

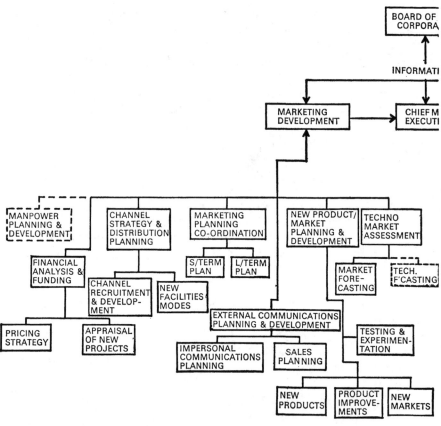

Figure D.11 THE FUTURE/PRESENT

ORGANIZATIONAL TRANSFER – ORGANIZATIONAL DEVELOPMENT

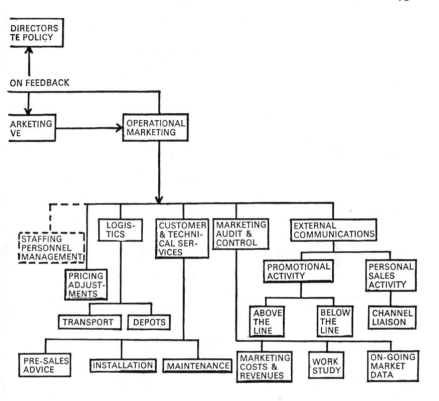

PATTERN OF MARKETING TASKS

176 ORGANIZATIONAL DESIGN FOR MARKETING FUTURES

SELECTED BIBLIOGRAPHY: PART D

Bright, J. R., *Technological Forecasting for Industry and Government: Methods and Applications*, Prentice-Hall, 1968.

Christopher, M. G., Magrill, L., and Wills, G. S. C., 'Educational Development for Marketing Logistics', *International Journal of Physical Distribution*, 1, 2, 1971.

Christopher, M. G., and Wills, G. S. C. (eds), *Marketing Logistics and Distribution Planning*, Allen and Unwin, 1972.

Cowan, D. S., and Jones, R. W., *Advertising in the 21st Century*, Hutchinson, 1968.

Futures, a quarterly journal from Iliffe Scientific and Technical Books Ltd.

Galbraith, J. K., *The New Industrial State*, Hamish Hamilton, 1967; Penguin, 1969.

Goldman, P., 'Consumerism: Art or Science?', *Journal of Royal Society of Arts*, 1969, Vol. 117, August.

Haldane, I., 'ESOMAR Proceedings', reprinted in Seibert, J., and Wills, G. S. C. (eds), *Marketing Research*, Penguin, 1970.

International Journal of Physical Distribution, published thrice-yearly by IPC Transport Press.

Johns, E. A., 'The Use of Tests in the Selection of Salesmen', *British Journal of Marketing*, 2, 3, pp. 185–99.

Journal of Long Range Planning, published quarterly by Pergamon Press.

Kahn, H., and Wiener, A. J., *The Year 2000*, Macmillan, 1968.

Kelley, W. T., *Marketing Intelligence: the Management of Marketing Information*, Staples Press, 1968.

Kotler, P., *Marketing Audit and Control* (Seminar Manual), University of Bradford Management Centre, 1969.

Mayer, M. S., and Suiden, G., *Trends in Canadian Marketing*, Queen's Printer, Ottawa, 1967.

O'Shaughnessy, J., *Work Study Applied to a Sales Force*, B.I.M., 1965.

Sevin, C. H., *Marketing Productivity Analysis*, McGraw-Hill, 1965.

Taylor, B., and Wills, G. S. C. (eds), *Long Range Planning for Marketing and Diversification*, Crosby Lockwood for Bradford University Press, 1971.

Taylor, B., and Wills, G. S. C. (eds), *Pricing Strategy*, Staples Press, 1969.

Tookey, D., and McDougall, C., *The Exporters*, Ashridge Management College, 1969.

Wills, G. S. C., 'Cost–Benefit Analysis of a Test Market', in *Marketing Research*, edited by Seibert, J., and Wills, G. S. C., Penguin, 1970.

Wills, G. S. C., *Exploration in Marketing Thought*, Crosby Lockwood for Bradford University Press, 1971.

Wills, G. S. C., *Technological Forecasting: The Art and its Managerial Implications*, Penguin, 1971.

Wills, G. S. C., Ashton, D. J. L., and Taylor, B. (eds), *Technological Forecasting and Corporate Strategy*, Crosby Lockwood for Bradford University Press, 1969.

Wills, G. S. C., and Christopher, M. G., 'The Cost Benefit Analysis of External Information: Some Theoretical Approaches', *UNESCO Library Bulletin*, January 1970.

APPENDIX I

RESEARCH METHODOLOGY EMPLOYED IN SURVEY OF COMPANIES

The universe was defined as all companies in the United Kingdom which, on the most recent figures available, had an annual turnover of three-quarters of a million pounds or more. A list of all firms which met this criterion was obtained from the then Board of Trade and consisted of 2,400 companies. It was decided that all firms in this list should be approached to provide information at some stage in the research.

Two hundred firms, selected by a random interval procedure, were asked to co-operate in the first stage of the research by allowing a senior executive to be interviewed by trained interviewers. A great deal of information was obtained from the 67 firms who consented to this, on the basis of which we constructed the questionnaire which was administered on a postal basis. A copy of this questionnaire is reproduced in Appendix 2.

From the complete list of 2,400 companies we deleted the 200 which had been approached in the first stage of qualitative interviews. A further 310 firms had to be excluded from the mailing list either because no reliable address could be found or they had ceased trading.

Questionnaires were therefore sent to the remaining 1,890 firms on the Board of Trade list; thus we were aiming to carry out a census of all appropriate firms. A covering letter, routed to the chief executive, explained the purpose of the survey and contained an assurance that the information provided would be treated as confidential. Subsequently, two reminders were sent to non-respondents; on both occasions a further questionnaire was enclosed.

A total of 1,063 (56 per cent) of the companies approached replied to our letters. Of these, 553 completed and returned questionnaires which were usable. A further 312 firms explained that they had not completed the questionnaire because it was not applicable to their situation. The major reasons given for this were that they were re-organizing their activities internally, were merging with another

178   APPENDIX I

company or that they were holding companies where the marketing function was carried out by subsidiaries. The final reason was that they judged the questionnaire to be irrelevant to their business activity; responses in this area normally indicated that marketing had not been established formally within the firm.

Letters were received from 198 firms who, although not finding the questionnaire irrelevant to their business activity, refused to complete the questionnaire. The principal reasons for refusal were concerned with the time and effort involved, and very few replies indicated a lack of sympathy or hostility to the objectives of the survey.

A 5 per cent telephone check was made on the firms who did not reply at all; these firms explained their non-response in the same terms as the reasons stated above for inapplicability or refusal.

APPENDIX 2

SURVEY QUESTIONNAIRES ON THE MARKET ORGANIZATIONAL STATUS QUO

SURVEY OF MARKETING ORGANIZATION STRUCTURES
IN THE UNITED KINGDOM (BY POST)

12. Could you please state the precise title of the executive with main responsibility for marketing (Chief Marketing Executive).

Sales Director	1
Commercial Director	2
Marketing Director	3
Managing Director	4
Sales Manager	5
Marketing Manager	6
Any other (*please specify*)—	

....

....

13. For which of the following functions has the Chief Marketing Executive full responsibility, shared responsibility or no responsibility?

	Full Responsi- bility	Shared Responsi- bility	No Responsi- bility	Not Applicable
14. Sales Forecasting	1	2	3	4
Marketing Research	5	6	7	8
15. Advertising and Promotion	1	2	3	4
Overseas Marketing	5	6	7	8
16. Pricing	1	2	3	4
Physical Distribution	5	6	7	8
17. Packaging	1	2	3	4
Public Relations	5	6	7	8
18. Marketing Staff Selection and Training	1	2	3	4
New Product Planning	5	6	7	8

20. Does your Company have a written-down organisation chart?

Yes 1   No 2

21. In relation to the Chief Production Executive is the Chief Marketing Executive—

Of equal status? 1   Of lower status? 2   Of higher status? 3

179

180 APPENDIX 2

22. What are the titles of the personnel reporting directly to the Chief Marketing Executive?

23. How many people are employed in the marketing area? ☐

24. How many of the total employed in the marketing area are full-time marketing executives? ☐

25. How many of the total employed in the marketing area are members of the sales force? ☐

26. Do any marketing executives have written-down job specifications?

Yes 1 No 2

(*If yes*). Is it general company policy to have written-down job specifications for all company executives?

Yes 4 No 5

27. Do you break your marketing activities down—

(a) according to products in your range?	Yes	1	No	2
(b) according to geographic area?	Yes	3	No	4
(c) according to customers?	Yes	5	No	6
(d) according to any combination of the above?	Yes	7	No	8

28. (e) in any other way? (*please specify*) Yes 1 No 2

Many firms use external agencies to assist them in carrying out a part or all of a number of marketing activities. Will you please say whether you use external agencies either partly or entirely in respect of the functions listed—

	Partly/ Occa- sionally	Entirely	Not used	Not Appro- priate
29. Display/Pack Design	1	2	3	4
Advertising	5	6	7	8
30. Marketing Research	1	2	3	4
Public Relations	5	6	7	8
31. Transport of finished goods	1	2	3	4
Sales Operations	5	6	7	8
32. Customer Credit/H.P.	1	2	3	4

33. Has the Chief Marketing Executive ever attended any educational courses in marketing either before or after joining your company?

Yes 1 No 2

Appendix 2

181

Which of these methods of promotion do you employ to sell your products?
(*For all promotional methods used, we should be grateful if you could indicate the approximate proportion of the promotional budget that each represents*).

		Used	Not used	% of Total Promotion
34.	Personal selling	1	2	
35.	Above the line advertising	1	2	
36.	Below the line advertising	1	2	
37.	Direct mail	1	2	
38.	Exhibitions	1	2	
39.	Public relations	1	2	

Any other (*please specify*)—

40. ....

41. ....

42. ....

43. Approximately what proportion of gross sales revenue did your total promotional expenditure represent in the last financial year?

Under 1%	1	1%–2.9%	2
3%–4.9%	3	5%–10%	4
Over 10%	5		

44. On what basis do you determine the amount to be spent on advertising?

Percentage of past sales	1
Percentage of expected sales	2
Percentage of profit	3
Other (*please specify*)	

....

45. On what basis do you generally fix your prices?

"Cost plus"	1
"Cost plus" modified by market conditions	2
Market conditions	3
Any other (*please specify*)—	

46. What are the major factors considered in selecting the channels of distribution you use?

47. Which of the following distribution channels do you use?

Wholesalers	1
Retailers	2
Direct to users	3
Agents/Brokers	4
Other	5

48. For what periods ahead does your company develop forecasts for total company sales?

Less than one year	1
1 year and less than 3 years	2
3 years and less than 5 years	3
5 years and less than 10 years	4
10 years and over	5

APPENDIX 2

49. Does your company have written-down marketing plans?

         Yes   1   No   2

(If yes). For what periods?

Less than one year	4
1 year and less than 3 years	5
3 years and less than 5 years	6
5 years and less than 10 years	7
10 years and over	8

50. What are the principal headings of your current marketing plan?

51. Which senior executives participate in the preparation of your marketing plans?

Chief Executive	1
Chief Marketing Executive	2
Chief Production Executive	3
Head of Research and Development	4
Chief Finance Executive	5
Others *(please specify)*—	

....

....

52. Do you ever carry out any marketing research activities?

         Yes   1   No   2

(If no, please proceed to Question 82 on page 5)

(If yes). Does anyone in the company have full-time responsibility for marketing research?

53.   Yes   1   No   2

(If yes). What is his/her precise job title?

(If no, proceed to Question 56)

Market Research Manager	4
Market Research Officer	5
Any other *(please specify)*—	

....

....

54. Does he/she have a written-down job specification?

         Yes   1   No   2

55. How long has the company had someone responsible for marketing research on a full-time basis?

Less than one year	1
1 year and less than 3	2
3 years and less than 5	3
5 years and less than 10	4
10 years and over	5

56. To whom is the senior marketing researcher responsible in your company?

57. What was the total cost of marketing research activities in your last financial year?

APPENDIX 2

58. Have you ever tested new products by marketing them in a restricted geographical area?
(*If yes*). What percentage of your new products are tested in this way?

%

Which of the following marketing research activities were carried out either by your own personnel or an external agency during 1968?

	Not	Internal	External	Both
59. Studies of acceptability and potential of new products	1	2	3	4
Studies of present products versus competition	5	6	7	8
60. Packaging research and design	1	2	3	4
Research on competitors' products	5	6	7	8
61. Product testing, blind product tests	1	2	3	4
Assessment of market potential	5	6	7	8
62. Determination of market characteristics	1	2	3	4
Market share analysis	5	6	7	8
63. Studies of market changes (geographic, age-distribution, etc.)	1	2	3	4
Sales analysis	5	6	7	8
64. Establishment of sales quotas	1	2	3	4
Establishment of sales territories	5	6	7	8
65. Studies of effectiveness of methods of paying salesmen	1	2	3	4
Analysis of effectiveness of channels of distribution	5	6	7	8
66. Distribution cost studies	1	2	3	4
Test marketing	5	6	7	8
67. Retail audits	1	2	3	4
Measuring effectiveness of special offers	5	6	7	8
68. Copy research	1	2	3	4
Media studies	5	6	7	8

What proportion of your total marketing research expenditure went on specific areas of marketing activity last year?

69.	Product	.... %
70.	Market	.... %
71.	Sales including distribution	.... %
72.	Advertising and promotion	.... %
73.	Others	.... %

We have examined your marketing research activities in terms of the data they generate.
Could you now please, describe the most important *techniques* you use in terms of expenditure on each as a proportion of your total research expenditure?

74.	Qualitative Research	.... %
75.	Trade/Retail Audits	.... %
76.	Customer Panels	.... %

184 APPENDIX 2

77.	Continuous Surveys	.... %
78.	Ad hoc Surveys	.... %
79.	Experimentation	.... %
	Others (*please specify*)—	
80.	....	.... %
81.	....	.... %

Below are a number of statements which have been made about some aspects of business activity.

Please indicate the extent to which you agree or disagree with each statement by circling the appropriate response. A space is provided for any comments you may wish to make:

---

82. "The marketing man's job is simply to sell what the works produce."

Strongly Agree   Agree   Undecided   Disagree   Strongly Disagree

Further Comment:

---

83. "Our main task is to increase sales volume. Profits will follow naturally."

Strongly Agree   Agree   Undecided   Disagree   Strongly Disagree

Further Comment:

---

84. "A well made product will sell itself."

Strongly Agree   Agree   Undecided   Disagree   Strongly Disagree

Further Comment:

---

85. "Further increases in profitability will be attained mainly by more efficient production."

Strongly Agree   Agree   Undecided   Disagree   Strongly Disagree

Further Comment:

---

86. "Diversification policies should build on existing company resources."

Strongly Agree   Agree   Undecided   Disagree   Strongly Disagree

Further Comment:

---

87. "Provided we succeed in selling a planned level of production, we should not be too concerned with trends in the total market."

Strongly Agree   Agree   Undecided   Disagree   Strongly Disagree

Further Comment:

---

88. "In our type of business we know the market too well to need marketing research."

Strongly Agree   Agree   Undecided   Disagree   Strongly Disagree

Further Comment:

APPENDIX 2

4. What do you understand by the term "marketing"?

5. What implications do you think developments in marketing will have for the way you organize your activities in the next 10 to 15 years?

CLASSIFICATION DATA

1. Size in terms of total number of people employed.

Up to 249	1
250–499 people	2
500–999 people	3
1,000–2,999 people	4
3,000–4,999 people	5
5,000 and over	6

2. Size in terms of Gross Sales Revenue during last financial year.

Below £1 m.	1
£1 m.–4.9 m.	2
£5 m.–9.9 m.	3
£10 m.–24.9 m.	4
£25 m.–49.9 m.	5
£50 m. or over	6

3. Nature of business activity.

Manufacturer of Consumer Products	1
Manufacturer of Industrial Products	2
Distribution	3
Services	4

THANK YOU FOR YOUR HELP

186   APPENDIX 2

RAS 2439(MOS)   Serial No. ———

RESEARCH & AUDITING SERVICES LTD
'Randas House' 5–11 Westway
London W.12

BRITISH INSTITUTE OF MANAGEMENT & UNIVERSITY OF BRADFORD MANAGEMENT CENTRE

Survey of Marketing Organisation Structures in British Industry – Director: Professor Gordon Wills

Thank you for sparing some of your time to see me. I am working for the University of Bradford Research team to assist with the fieldwork for their joint survey with the B I M of marketing organisation structures in British industry.

1   I should like, if I may, to begin by making an exact note of your job title as Chief Marketing Executive.

Sales Director	1
Commercial Director	2
Marketing Director	3
Sales Manager	4
Marketing Manager	5

(SPECIFY)————————————————Any other

(PLEASE ALSO RECORD EXACT NAME AND ADDRESS OF THE COMPANY CONCERNED)

Company name————————————

Postal address in full ————————————

————————————

————————————

SECTION ONE

The questionnaire is divided into four sections. In the first, I should like to ask a number of questions about your own personal background and career history.

2   How long have you held your present position in this company? (IN YEARS)

3   (a) Prior to taking up this present appointment, what was the full title of the job you held?

3   (b) Was that with this company (or group) or elsewhere?

Present company	1
Elsewhere	2

IF "ELSEWHERE"

3   (c) With what company was that?

APPENDIX 2

RAS 2439(MOS)

4 Will you briefly describe for me the pattern of your earlier career development since you finished full-time education?

PROBE – ENSURE THAT ANY JOBS IN DIFFERENT BUSINESS FUNCTIONS ARE FULLY LISTED

5 (a) Has your career included any periods of management education?

Yes	1
No	2

IF "YES"

5 (b) Would you briefly describe the course(s) you have attended?

TYPE/CONTENT	WHERE	WHEN	LENGTH

5 (c) Did any of these result in any formal professional qualifications or degrees of any sort?

Yes	1
No	2

IF "YES"
What are they?

5 (d) Finally, will you very briefly describe your educational background before you embarked on a business-career?

6 (a) Returning again now to your present job, do you have any *written* terms of reference or job specification?

Yes	1
No	2

188 APPENDIX 2

RAS 2439(MOS)

    IF "YES"

    We should very much like, if possible, to have a copy of them.
    May I have one please?

Yes	1
No	2

    IF "NO" OR NONE EXIST, ASK

6 (b) Will you briefly describe what your terms of reference are / how
    you see them?

SHOW CARD A

7 On this card is a list of management functions. I would like to ask you to say
for each in turn as I read them out, whether you have FULL, SHARED or NO
RESPONSIBILITY for it in your company. Sometimes the functions may be
inappropriate for your company altogether. If this is so, please say so.

APPENDIX 2 189

RAS 2439(MOS)

CHECK METHOD UNDERSTOOD AND THEN READ EACH ONE OUT IN TURN IN THE ORDER LISTED

	FULL	SHARED	NONE	INAPPROPRIATE
Customer relations	1	2	3	4
Sales forecasting	1	2	3	4
Marketing research	1	2	3	4
Advertising	1	2	3	4
Exporting	1	2	3	4
International marketing	1	2	3	4
Pricing	1	2	3	4
Product planning	1	2	3	4
Factory stock levels of finished goods	1	2	3	4
Warehousing	1	2	3	4
Transport of finished goods	1	2	3	4
Packaging	1	2	3	4
Product design	1	2	3	4
Public relations	1	2	3	4
Diversification studies	1	2	3	4
Sales volume	1	2	3	4
Discount structures	1	2	3	4
Customer credit policies	1	2	3	4
Direct mail	1	2	3	4
Below the line promotion	1	2	3	4
Marketing staff selection	1	2	3	4
Marketing training	1	2	3	4

190   APPENDIX 2

RAS 2439(MOS)

Are there any functions we have omitted for which you have full or shared responsibility as the Chief Marketing Executive?

IF "YES"

What are they?

	FULL	SHARED
	1	2
	1	2

SECTION TWO

In the second section, I have some questions on the way in which you organise the company and in particular, the marketing function.

8 (a) Does your company have a *written down* organisation chart?

Yes	1
No	2

IF "YES"

We should very much like, if possible, to have a copy of it. May I have one please?

Yes	1
No	2

IF "NO" OR NONE EXISTS

PASS SHEET B TO RESPONDENT AND ASK

8 (b) Will you please sketch the framework of your organisation from the Chief Executive downwards. In particular, will you show how the marketing activities relate to one another, to other functions of the business, and to yourself.

NOTE TO INTERVIEWER – WE DO NOT WANT NAMES OF JOB OCCU-PANTS BUT OF THE JOBS THEY CARRY OUT. ASK ALL RESPONDENTS WHETHER CHART SKETCHED OR PROVIDED

8 (c) Will you please indicate on the chart the number of full-time employees of all descriptions who work in each area of the marketing activity described. Please write the number next to each relevant level on the chart (rough estimates will suffice).

8 (d) We are particularly concerned to ensure that on your chart the relative status of the chief executives in each functional area is adequately indicated. Do you feel this point has been taken care of?

Yes	1
No	2

IF "NO"

Would you please adjust it?

Appendix 2 191

RAS 2439(MOS)

PROBE – WHAT JOB TITLES DO THE OTHER FUNCTIONAL CHIEF
EXECUTIVES HAVE? (WRITE IN ON CHART IN FULL)

8 (e) Many firms use external agencies to assist them in carrying out either a
part, or all of a number of marketing activities.

SHOW CARD C

Will you please say whether you use external agencies either partly or
entirely in respect of the functions listed.

READ OUT FUNCTIONS ONE BY ONE

	PARTLY/ OCCASIONALLY	ENTIRELY	NOT USED
Product design	1	2	3
Display / Pack design	1	2	3
Advertising (above the line)	1	2	3
Merchandising	1	2	3
Marketing Research	1	2	3
Public relations	1	2	3
Transport of finished goods	1	2	3
Diversification studies	1	2	3
Sales Operations	1	2	3
Customer credit / H P	1	2	3
Marketing staff selection	1	2	3
Marketing training	1	2	3

Are there any areas we have omitted in which you have used external
agencies at all as chief marketing executive?

IF "YES"

What are they?

	PARTLY / OCCASIONALLY	ENTIRELY	NOT USED
	1	2	3
	1	2	3

192 APPENDIX 2

RAS 2439(MOS)

SECTION THREE

In the third section of this questionnaire, I should like to turn to some specific questions about how the organisation structure you have described operates.

9   For what period(s) ahead does your company develop sales forecasts?

PROBE — MANY FIRMS WILL DEVELOP FORECASTS FOR A RANGE OF DIFFERENT TIMES — PROBE TO SECURE ALL PERIODS AHEAD

10   Does your company then proceed to develop a plan for the various levels of marketing activity felt necessary to achieve these forecasts?

Yes	1
No	2

IF "NO"

How does your company seek to achieve forecast levels of sales?

11   What are the main headings you have developed in your current marketing plan?

12   Who participated, both from within and without the 'marketing area' in your company, in the development of your current plan?

PROBE FULLY

13 (a) At what stages, if at all, in the marketing planning process, do you expect non-marketing personnel to be involved?

13 (b) What contribution do they make?

APPENDIX 2   193

RAS 2439(MOS)

13 (c) How do you set about working with them?	
14 When your marketing planning has been completed within the marketing area, in what way are your proposals digested, modified, and/or acted upon within the company as a whole? PROBE FULLY	
15 In what ways within the marketing function do you seek to *co-ordinate* the various activities in the marketing plan, in order to achieve sales forecasts? PROBE – COMMITTEES, PROJECT GROUPS ETC. – GET NOMEN-CLATURE EMPLOYED	
16 What methods of *control* within the marketing area do you employ in order to monitor progress towards your sales forecasts? PROBE FULLY	

17 Do you *review* your product range on a regular basis?		
	Yes	1
	No	2
IF 'NO' When was it last reviewed?		

N

194 APPENDIX 2

RAS 2439(MOS)

IF 'YES'
How frequently do you review it?

18 (a) What methods do you employ for evaluating *existing* products?
PROBE FULLY

18 (b) What criteria do you employ for the *deletion* of products from your existing range?
PROBE FULLY

18 (c) What criteria do you employ for the *introduction of new products* into your range?
PROBE FULLY

18 (d) On the last occasion when you introduced a new product, what particular research techniques did you use?
PROBE FULLY

APPENDIX 2

RAS 2439(MOS)

19	What criteria do you employ for diversification of your company's business into *new* markets using *new* products? PROBE FULLY	
20 (a)	What major factors did you take into account in deciding the prices you charge for your products? PROBE FULLY	
20 (b)	What methods do you employ for reviewing your prices?	
21 (a)	What major factors did you take into account in selecting the channels of distribution which you use? PROBE FULLY	
21 (b)	What channels do you use? PROBE FULLY	
21 (c)	What methods do you employ for reviewing your channels?	

196 APPENDIX 2

RAS 2439(MOS)

SHOW CARD D

22 (a) Which of these methods of promotion do you employ to sell your products?

22 (b) What proportion of your total promotional budget goes to each of these forms of activity, in value terms, as a percentage of the total?

| | Q. 22 (a) | | Q. 22 (b) |
	USED	NOT USED	%
Personal selling	1	2	
Above the line advertising	1	2	
Below the line advertising	1	2	
Direct mail	1	2	
Exhibitions	1	2	
Public relations	1	2	
Any other (*please specify*)			
			100%

23 Roughly speaking, what was your *total* promotional spending during your last financial year, as a percentage of gross sales revenue?

Less than 1%	1
1 but under 3%	2
3 but under 5%	3
5 but under 10%	4
10% and over	5

24 (a) What criteria did you employ in deciding the size of your *total* promotional expenditure during the current year?

PROBE FULLY

APPENDIX 2   197

RAS 2439(MOS)

24 (b) What criteria did you use in deciding how to allocate the total budget in the terms you have just described at Q.22 (b) ? **PROBE FULLY**	
25 (a) What criteria did you use in deciding the size of your current annual appropriation for marketing research ? **PROBE FULLY**	
25 (b) What proportion of gross sales revenue did the total marketing research appropriation represent during the last financial year? **PROBE FULLY**	
25 (c) How are marketing research investigations initiated in your company? **PROBE FULLY**	

198 APPENDIX 2

RAS 2439(MOS)

25 (d) How does your company try to ensure that it gets the most benefit from the findings of marketing research?

25 (e) What criteria do you use in deciding whether specific piece of marketing research is likely to be worthwhile or not? PROBE FULLY

SECTION FOUR

The final section is very brief. I would like to ask just one or two brief questions on the development of marketing in the company.

26 Can you, in brief, describe how and why marketing emerged in your company in the particular way it stands today?

PROBE – IN PARTICULAR, CAN YOU DETAIL THE ORGANISA-TIONAL PATTERN FOR MARKETING PRIOR TO THE EXISTING STRUCTURE, AND INDICATE HOW AND WHY IT HAS CHANGED?

35 Can you tell me briefly, what you think the marketing concept means *for your company*, both now and in the future? NOW

APPENDIX 2 199

RAS 2439(MOS)

IN THE FUTURE

CLASSIFICATION DATA

That is the end of the formal questions. I should like finally, to secure some classification data as the basis for our analysis of all the replies we receive. Could you please complete the details on this sheet – SHOW SHEET E – *When returned, staple to questionnaire (after the organisational structure where sketched)*.

NOTE TO INTERVIEWERS

THE QUESTIONNAIRE MUST BE MATCHED AND ATTACHED TO THE QUESTIONNAIRE FOR THE 'MARKETING RESEARCH MANAGER' FOR THE ORGANISATION.

200 APPENDIX 2

RAS 2439(MR)   Serial No————

RESEARCH & AUDITING SERVICES LTD
'Randas House' 5–11 Westway
London W.12

BRITISH INSTITUTE OF MANAGEMENT & UNIVERSITY OF BRADFORD MANAGEMENT CENTRE

Survey of Marketing Research in British Industry

Thank you for sparing some of your time to see me. I am working for the University of Bradford research team to assist with the fieldwork for their joint survey with the B I M of 'marketing research in British industry'.

For the purpose of this survey, marketing research is defined as:

(SHOW CARD F AND READ OUT THE DEFINITION).

The objective gathering, recording and analysing of all facts about problems relating to the creation, development, transfer and sales of goods and services from producer to consumer.
If fact finding methods meet the above criteria, then this will be considered to be marketing research, no matter who does it. It may be done by a Marketing Research Department, by some other department in the firm, or even by no department at all, but by an individual or outside agency.

1 (a) Might I begin by asking you your precise job title?

1 (b) Are you employed full-time in the marketing research activity within the company?

Yes   1
No   2

IF NOT FULL-TIME

1 (c) What other responsibilities do you have?

IF FULL-TIME EMPLOYED IN MARKETING RESEARCH

1 (d) When was the first man or woman appointed full-time to supervise marketing research activities in the company?

2 (a) Will you please outline briefly the terms of reference you have in your job within the marketing research area?

APPENDIX 2

RAS 2439(MR)

2 (b) Will you briefly describe how marketing research has developed in your company since its ingestion?

2 (c) Will you briefly describe your own career since completing full-time education, both within and without this company?

2 (d) Have you attended any educational courses since you embarked on your business careers either in marketing research or any allied subject?

| | Yes | 1 |
| | No | 2 |

IF 'YES'

What were they?

TYPE/CONTENT	WHERE	WHEN	DURATION OF COURSE

Did any formal qualification result?

| | Yes | 1 |
| | No | 2 |

IF 'YES'

What are they?

2 (e) Could you briefly describe your personal educational background prior to embarking on your career?

202   APPENDIX 2

RAS 2439(MR)

3   Will you please sketch on this sheet (HAND OVER SHEET G)
     the organisational pattern of marketing research in your
     company? Please show all the *main activities* such as field-
     work, data processing etc., if relevant as well as any other
     divisions of activity you may have. Please also show *contact
     points* with others both inside and external to your company
     who help carry through marketing research. There may, for
     instance, be work done by outside companies or by your
     advertising agency etc. Please indicate these by dotted lines.

     (ALLOW AMPLE TIME FOR THE CHART TO BE DRAWN)

4   Will you now please mark in on the chart the number of employees *within*
     the company involved at each point. Please write the number next to each
     activity. Will you divide the numbers as between

                   FULL-TIMERS and
                   PART-TIMERS
          and between
                   EXECUTIVE & MANAGERIAL, and
                   ALL OTHER GRADES.

5   Do you have any plans in the future for changing this pattern of
     marketing research organisation in your company?

                                                   Yes   I
                                                   No   2
     IF "YES"
     What are they, briefly?

6   Approximately how much was spent in 1968 (or your latest
     financial year) on marketing research, including salaries and all
     other expenses?
                                          £ ———

7   Of the above amount what proportion was spend on *outside*
     marketing research services commissioned? (Do *NOT* include
     such routine matters as preparation of charts and slides, photo-
     stats, etc. But *DO* include research studies done by others, con-
     tinuing research such as store audits, regular measurement of
     advertising readership, or purchased work of similar type).
                                          ———%

8   We are aware of the difficulty of estimating charges for market-
     ing research jobs done in other departments (accounting,
     statistical, etc.) but if you know the approximate total, and if it
     is *NOT* included under Question 6, how much was it?
                                          £ ———

APPENDIX 2

RAS 2439(MR)

9 (a) What criteria does your company use in deciding whether to get a research study conducted outside or internally?

9 (b) What criteria do you use in judging one external research contractor against another?

10 What planning process does your company go through in the marketing research area each year, in order to determine the annual marketing research appropriation?

11 (a) How are marketing research investigations initiated in your company?

11 (b) What guidelines are used in your company in the planning of marketing research investigation?

11 (c) What guidelines are used in their conduct?

11 (d) How do you exercise *control* during their conduct?

11 (e) How does your company try to ensure that it gets the most benefit from the findings of marketing research *once a job is completed*?

204 APPENDIX 2

RAS 2439(MR)

11 (f) Do research reports contain recommendations for action?

	Yes	I
	No	2

IF "YES"

11 (g) Are such recommendations acted on?

	Yes	I
	No	2
	sometimes	3

11 (h) What criteria do you use in evaluating before the event, whether a given piece of research will be worth its cost?

12 (a) In what way, if any, is the marketing research viewpoint (either through yourself or others in the area) 'represented' in the executive marketing function of your company? (Please describe any formal or informal procedures, e.g. committees, task groups, etc.)

12 (b) In which of these areas of your business (*SHOW CARD H*) do you think marketing research is nearly always, frequent, occasionally, seldom if ever influential?

	Nearly always	Frequently	Occasionally	Seldom if ever
a) Product development	I	2	3	4
b) Packaging	I	2	3	4
c) Pricing	I	2	3	4
d) Distribution	I	2	3	4
e) Promotion and advertising	I	2	3	4
f) Production levels	I	2	3	4
g) Public relations	I	2	3	4

Are there any other areas where marketing research has some measure of influence which I have not mentioned?

APPENDIX 2 205

RAS 2439(MR)
IF "YES"
What are they?

	Nearly always	Frequently	Occasionally	Seldom if ever
	1	2	3	4
	1	2	3	4
	1	2	3	4

13   Has any member of the marketing research department been at any time, promoted to a general or like management position?

Yes   1
No   2

IF "YES"
Please describe the most recent incident

14   On this card (*SHOW CARD J*) is a list of various types of marketing research which your company might have undertaken *during 1968*. I shall read out each in turn and I should like you to tell me whether anything was done and if so, whether it was done externally, internally, or both.

In order to establish some minimum for comparative purposes, please answer only for those activities where at least some fact-finding research took place and a written report was submitted to someone outside the marketing research department. This excludes statements of opinion and memoranda, sometimes requested by management.

	NOT DONE	INTERNAL	EXTERNAL	BOTH
PRODUCT RESEARCH a) Studies of acceptability of new products and potential	1	2	3	4
b) Studies of present products versus competition	1	2	3	4
c) Packaging research, design or physical characteristics	1	2	3	4
d) Research on competitors' products	1	2	3	4
e) Product testing, blind product tests	1	2	3	4

206   APPENDIX 2

RAS 2439(MR)

	NOT DONE	INTERNAL	EXTERNAL	BOTH
f) Other product research (*please specify*)	I	2	3	4
MARKET RESEARCH g) Development of market potentials	I	2	3	4
h) Determination of market characteristics	I	2	3	4
i) 'Share of the Market' analyses	I	2	3	4
j) Studies of market changes (geographic, age-distribution etc).	I	2	3	4
k) Sales analysis	I	2	3	4
l) Other (*please explain*)	I	2	3	4
SALES RESEARCH m) Establishment of sales quotas	I	2	3	4
n) Establishment of sales territories	I	2	3	4
o) Studies of effectiveness of methods of paying salesmen (incentive scheme)	I	2	3	4
p) Analysis of effectiveness of channels of distribution	I	2	3	4
q) Distribution cost studies	I	2	3	4
r) Test marketing	I	2	3	4
rr) Retail Audits	I	2	3	4
s) Premiums, studies of 'deals'	I	2	3	4
t) Other (*please explain*)	I	2	3	4

APPENDIX 2

RAS 2439(MR)

	NOT DONE	INTERNAL	EXTERNAL	BOTH
ADVERTISING RESEARCH				
u) Copy research	1	2	3	4
v) Media studies	1	2	3	4
w) Use of projective techniques 'motivation' research	1	2	3	4
x) Other (*please explain*)	1	2	3	4
BUSINESS ECONOMICS				
y) Short-range forecasting (up to one year)	1	2	3	4
z) Long-range forecasting (more than one year)	1	2	3	4
aa) Forecasting of personnel requirements (this includes all personnel affected by changes in sales volume)	1	2	3	4
bb) Studies of business trends	1	2	3	4
cc) Profit analysis	1	2	3	4
dd) Plant and warehouse locations	1	2	3	4
ee) Purchase of companies foreign productive facilities	1	2	3	4
ff) Other (*please explain*)	1	2	3	4
EXPORT MARKETING RESEARCH				
gg) Product research	1	2	3	4
hh) Market research	1	2	3	4
ii) Sales research including distribution	1	2	3	4
jj) Advertising research	1	2	3	4
kk) Business economics	1	2	3	4

208   APPENDIX 2

RAS 2439(MR)

15   What proportion of your total marketing research expenditure went on specific areas of marketing activity last year?

SHOW CARD K

Product	———%
Market	———%
Sales including distribution	———%
Advertising & Promotion	———%
Business Economics	———%
Others (*Please specify*)	
———————————————	———%
———————————————	———%
———————————————	———%
	100 %

16   We have examined your marketing research activities in terms of the data they generate. Could you now please, describe the most important *techniques* you use in terms of expenditure on each as a proportion of your total research expenditure?

SHOW CARD L

Qualitative Research	———%
Trade/Retail Audits	———%
Customer Panels	———%
Continuous Surveys	———%
Ad hoc surveys	———%
Experimentation	———%
Others (*please specify*)	
———————————————	———%
———————————————	———%
———————————————	———%
	100 %

APPENDIX 3

SELECTION OF DEFINITIONS OF MARKETING PROVIDED

In Response to Question: *'What do you understand by the term "marketing"?'*

1. The entire concept of integrated activities including sales, service, advertising, research and sales organization.

2. Identifying the customers needs relative to our products and providing goods to meet these needs.

3. Discovering user needs and satisfying these profitably in the markets in which we operate.

4. See Institute of Marketing handbook – can't improve on that.

5. To deliver consumer satisfaction at a profit.

6. Product selection, assessment, market location, servicing, distribution and profit awareness in terms of cost and margins. All in conjunction with other members of the executive team.

7. The bringing of goods or services from manufacturer or service company to the consumer or user.

8. The entire process of developing new products, pricing, promoting, market research, sales training, cost/efficiency in selling, advertising, direct mail, public relations.

9. To get the product the market demands in the right place at the right price at the right time and keep it that way.

10. Marketing is an embracing term covering market analysis, production planning, packaging, distribution, selling, advertising, public relations etc.

11. It is the whole process of determining consumer needs within given markets (or segments thereof) and then ensuring that the best possible product is made available to all potential customers at a competitive price offering real value to the consumer and a reasonable profit to manufacturer and distributor.

12. Planned selling.

13. The co-ordination of all corporate activity towards achievement of long term profit goals by satisfying market demands economically.

14. Marketing is the art of selling out what the consumer has sold in.

15. The 'total resources' concept, i.e. the offering of the total resources of an organization.

16. Satisfaction of consumer needs at maximum achievable rate of return.

17. A total business activity.

APPENDIX 3

18. Detailed study of all aspects of selling.

19. Marketing covers all operations in the process of causing goods to move from where they are manufactured to the hands of the ultimate user (except physical transportation). Included are marketing research, product selection and design, selection and methods of distribution, personal selling, advertising and other promotion methods, pricing and planning of overall market strategy.

20. It is almost the whole business operation. It is the assessment of what to sell in order to use the specialized skills of our staff, and also our manufacturing facilities to the best, most profitable advantage now and in the future and to promote sales accordingly.

21. Selling one's product in the market which produces the greatest profit in the long term.

22. Distribution to retailers.

23. Marketing is the link between supply and demand.

24. Promotion of little known or new products.

25. Sales promotion.

26. I don't know.

27. Marketing is as much an attitude as a definable function. This attitude linked with clear objectives based on a sound market intelligence creates a purposeful atmosphere which in turn generates a more dynamic approach at all levels.

28. Selling in the right place at the right time for the most profit.

29. Identification and satisfaction of market needs.

30. The efficient selling of goods.

NAME INDEX

Ames, B. C., 62, 87
Anderson, R. G., 87
Ansoff, H. I., 147
Argyris, C., 46, 86
Arnfield, R., 56, 87
Ashton, D. J., 176
Aspley, J. C., 48, 87

Baker, M., 14, 87
Barnard, C. I., 50, 86
Barnes, M., 45
Blankenship, A. B., 70, 87
Bossard, J., 49, 86
Boulton, M., 53
Braam, T., 14, 87
Bright, J. R., 176
Brown, L. O., 69, 87
Buell, V. P., 63–6, 87
Bund, H., 87
Buskirk, R. H., 61, 64, 87

Carroll, J. W., 87
Castle, B., 36
Christopher, M. G., 141, 176
Corbin, A., 53, 86–7
Cowan, D. S., 176
Currill, D., 144

Dale, E., 86
Dickson, W. J., 86
Doyle, J. B., 70, 87
Drucker, P., 50, 86
Durant, W. C., 48

Felton, A. P., 87

Galbraith, J. K., 27, 39, 55, 87, 176
Gilbreth, F., 25, 49, 86
Goldman, P., 176
Goodwin, E., 86–7
Graicunas, V. A., 86

Haldane, I., 176
Harkness, J. C., 68, 87
Hayhurst, R., 154

Johns, E. A., 176
Jones, R. W., 176

Kahn, H., 176
Keith, R. J., 87
Kelley, W. T., 176
Kelly, J., 45
Kemp, A. V., 14, 87
Koch, E. G., 87
Kotler, P., 51, 86, 176

Lawrence, P. R., 87
Lazo, H., 53, 86–7
Levitt, T., 21
Lorsch, J. W., 86

McDougall, C., 47, 86, 89, 176
McNamara, R., 38
Magrill, L., 176
Mann, J., 14
March, J. G., 50, 86
Mauser, F., 67, 87
Mayer, M. S., 176
Maynard, H. B., 86
Mayo, E., 50
Miller, E. C., 87
Moore, D. G., 54, 87

O'Shaughnessy, J., 86, 176

Peterson, R. N., 75, 87
Pfiffner, J. N., 46, 86
Pugh, D., 45

Randall, C. B., 50, 86
Robinson, E., 87
Rodger, L. W., 53, 87

o*

211

NAME INDEX

Roethlisberger, F. J., 50, 86

Saddik, S., 14, 127
Salisbury, J., 87
Sevin, C. H., 176
Shaw, A. W., 24–5, 48, 86
Sherwood, F. P., 46, 86
Simon, H. A., 46, 50, 86
Slater, A., 154
Sloan, A. P., 48, 86
Smith, A., 52, 86
Stanton, W. J., 61, 64, 87
Suiden, G., 176

Taylor, B., 176
Taylor, F. W., 25, 48–9, 86
Tillman, R., 86
Tookey, D., 47, 86, 89, 176

Urwick, L., 49, 86

Waters, C. W., 50, 86
Weber, M., 47, 50, 86
Wiener, A. J., 176
Wills, G., 55, 176
Woodward, J., 47, 86

Young, E., 49, 86

SUBJECT INDEX

Ad hoc surveys, 125–6
Advertising, 95, 103–8. *See also* Promotion
  above-the-line, 104
  agencies, 42, 124
  research
    expenditure on, 124
Aesthetics, 41, 166
Agencies
  advertising, 42, 124
  external, 102–3
Air freight, 159
American Management Association, 71
Auditing control of marketing, 138–40

Barrington Associates Inc., 52, 87
Behaviour, rational, in organizations, 46
Behavioural science applications, 24
Board of Trade, 177
British Institute of Management marketing research study, 114
British Standards Institution, 37
Bureaucracy, 47

Centralization and decentralization, 48, 55, 57, 68
Chairs of Marketing, 170
Channels, *see* Distribution channels
Chief Distribution Executive, 158
Chief Marketing Executive, 92–8
  responsibilities, 94–8
  status, 93
  title, 92–3
Committees, importance of, 54
Communications
  breakdown in mass markets, 23
  chains of, 50
  customer to manufacturer, 150–2
  education and, 170–1
  ethics and, 165

  in product planning, 74
  organization charts and, 101
Company
  needs, 79–80
  philosophy, 77–8
    dominance by marketing, 21–3
  policy, 78
  structure
    definition, 48
    informal, 80
Competition, 40
  for status, 43–4
Computerization, 22–3
  as a fashion, 41
  marketing information, 155, 157
  warehousing, 26
Conglomerates, 21–2
Consultants, 43
Consumer
  goods, 42, 75
    distribution channels, 110
    marketing research, expenditure on, 120
    planning period, 112
    promotion, 105, 107
    use of techniques, 152
  influence, 36–40
  organization, 37–8
Consumer Council, 37–8
Consumerism, 149–52
Consumers' Association, 37–8
Containerization, 27
Continuous surveys, 125
Control, 21–2, 76–9
  centralized, 68
  design, 83–4
  operational marketing, 138–40
  systems, 49
  techniques, 84
Co-ordination, 84–5
  computerization, 22–3

213

214 SUBJECT INDEX

distribution, 158
marketing planning, 148–9
promotion, 141
Corporate planning, 115
backlash, 20–3, 138
Costs
defective goods, 150
distribution, 35, 159
market penetration, 27
promotion, 106–8
research, 124
Council of Industrial Design, 41
Creativity, 71
routine analysis and, 136–7
Custom building, 24, 32–3, 39
Customer, 149–52
backlash, 36–40
effects on marketing, 40
housewife motivation, 34
needs, 72
orientation, marketing structures, 63–4
panels, 125
response, 20
service filtration unit, 150

Data
bank, 154, 157
systems, 42
Decentralization, see Centralization
Department of Economic Affairs, 29
Design, 166–7
as a fashion, 41
Direct mail, 104
Distribution, 31–2, 96
chief executive, 158
costing, 159
costs, 35
rationalization, 25–6
research, expenditure on, 123
total approach, 157, 159–61
use of promotion, 105
Distribution channels, 48, 109–10
consumer goods, 110
industrial goods, 109–10
'seizures', 24
strategy, 160
Diversification in distribution, 160
Divisionalization, 57
of marketing organization, 64–7, 138

Economic Development Committees, 37

Education, 34, 36
effect on purchasing, 38
marketing, 67–71
Environment, 19–44
effect on organization, 47
future, 19–44
in the seventies, 32–6
influence of fifties and sixties, 32–6
Ethics, 164–6
code, 165–6
policy, 166
European Economic Community, 30
European Free Trade Area, 30
Executives
chief distribution, 158
chief marketing, 92–8
hours of work, 33
movement within marketing sector, 172–3
Exhibitions, 103–4, 106
Exporting, see International marketing

Fashions, 40–4
'Filtering' information, 150
Forecasting
futures, 19–44
project, 74
sales, 110–11
technological, 27, 144–5
Future environment, 19–44
Futures, 176

Habitat Shops, 41, 166
Holding company, 164
Horniblow, Cox-Freeman, 141
House styles, 166
Human
approach to management, 50
needs, 80–1, 85

Income, disposable, 33
Industrial
advertising, 42
customers, 40
design, 41
goods, 112
distribution channels, 109–10
marketing research, 115
promotion, 105
test-marketing, 121
parks, 42
purchasing, 152
Industrial Marketing Research Association, 115

Subject Index

Industrial Reorganization Corporation, 29
Industries, priorities in British, 29
Information, 42, 153–7
  cost–benefit analysis, 153–4
  flow, 154
  from customer, 150
  systems, 115–16
Institute of Purchasing and Supply, 39
Institutionalization of industrial customers, 40
Intelligence systems, 152–7
International
  marketing, 95, 162–4
  markets, 160, 161–4
  trading, 30–1
International Journal of Physical Distribution, 176

Job
  descriptions, 50
  satisfaction, 33
  specifications, 101
Journal of Long Range Planning, 176
Journal of Marketing, 56

Labour Reform Government 1964–70, 29
Law, ethics and, 165
Leisure, 33
Logistics, 140
  function, 161

Mail order, 33
Management
  acceptance of marketing concept, 90–1
  development, 83
  education, 93–4, 167–71
  human approach, 50
Management Centre, University of Bradford, studies, 14–15, 89–134
  methodology, 177–8
  questionnaires, 179–208
Manufacturers, loss of influence, 39
Market
  characteristics, effect on organization, 47
  penetration, 27
Marketing
  attitudes, 126–32
  auditing control, 138–40

chief executive, 92–8
concept, acceptance by British management, 90–1
department, 98–102
  personnel, 99
  size, 98–9
development, 142, 143–9
director, 92–3
  characteristics, 52
education, 167–71
fusion with technical development, 143–9
futures, 19–44
information systems, 115–16, 152–7
intelligence systems, 152–7
international, 31, 95, 162–4
operational, 135–43
organization
  history, 45–87
  present state, 89–134
orientation, 51, 53–6
personnel, 99
  titles, 100–1
planning, 19–44, 148–9, 169
plans
  content, 113
  written-down, 111–13
routinization of, 23
segmentation, 32
structure
  alternatives, 56–67
  changes in, 31
  concepts, 76–85
  evolution, 85
  functions, 65
  subsystems, 56, 67–76
Marketing research, 95, 114–26
  contract, 42
  department, 69–71
    variations in structure, 69–71, 101–2
  development in UK, 114–16
  executive
    contrasted with marketing manager, 73
    full-time, 117–18
    supervision of, 118–19
    title, 118
  expenditure, 119–20, 122–6
  growth, 114
  organization trends, 115
  profile of activities, 121–6
  status, 116

SUBJECT INDEX

Markets
  changing, 27
  mass, 23
Marks & Spencer Ltd, 39, 152, 166
Ministry of Technology, 29, 144

National Coal Board, 35
National Economic Development Office, 29
National Industrial Conference Board (US), 67, 87
Needs, 72
  company, 79–80
  human, 80–1, 85
  reading of, 40

Objectives, 46–7, 78–9
  marketing, 113
  promotional 104
Operational marketing, 135–43
Organization
  charts, 101
  definition, 46
  structure, 45
  theory, 47–56
Organizational
  design, 171–3
  development, 135–76
Orientation toward marketing concept, 132
Overseas, see International
'Own brands', 25

Packaging, 96, 160
  design, 166
Peak load-shedding, 26, 43
Personal selling, 103–4, 106, 141
Physical distribution, see Distribution
Physical Distribution Management (PDM), 157
Policy, see Company policy
Political factors, 32–6
Polytechnics, 171
Pricing, 95–6, 108–9
  market-oriented, 109
Problem
  orientation, 23–32
  solving, 55
Product
  description, legal control of, 37
  division in marketing structures, 59–62, 64
  formulations, ethics and, 165

innovation, 27, 71–3
  skills sub-contracted, 43
manager
  compared with marketing manager, 62
  in marketing structures, 60–1
orientation, marketing structures, 59–62
planning, 72–6, 96
  division of responsibilities, 75
research, expenditure on, 123
Production, 172
  orientation, 52–4
Project forecasting, 74
Promotion, 103–8, 141. See also Advertising
  below-the-line, 25, 104
  consumer goods, 105, 107
  cost-effectiveness, 107–8
  expenditure on, 106–8
  future trends, 25
  industrial goods, 105
  related to company size, 106
  research, expenditure on, 124
  responsibility for, 95
  restructuring, 148
Public
  relations, 43, 96, 104
  warehousing, 26
Purchasing, professionalism in, 38–9

Qualitative research, 125

Recommendations acted upon by management, 115
Regional
  orientation of marketing structures, 62–3
  rebirth, 35–6
Research and development, 27, 144, 172
Retail
  audits, 125
  chains, 63
Rewards, 72
Routines, resistance to, 135–7
Routinization, 135–43

Sales
  director, 92–3
  force, 67–9
    co-ordination, 67

SUBJECT INDEX

forecasting, 94, 110–11
in-home, 34
manager, responsibilities, 53
orientation, 51, 53
personal, 103–4, 106, 141
research, expenditure on, 123
Salesmen
number of, 99
transfer to marketing, 137
'Sampling' new products, 27
Savings, attitudes toward, 35
Scalar chain, 49
Scenario planning, 169
Scientists, 71–2
motivation, 72
supervision, 72
Selective Employment Tax, 34–5
Self service, reversal in trend, 33–4
Service, 149–52
changes in, 33
customer differential, 160
distribution, optimum level, 159
to customers, 149–52
Skills, development of, 83
Slack time, 145
Social factors, 32–6
Staff
promotion, 82
selection, 96, 141, 169
Staffing, 83
data bank, 157
international markets, 164
Sub-contracting, 26, 42–3, 103
Sub-optimization, 51

Systems
approach to marketing, 49
data, 42, 154
marketing information, 115–16, 152–7

Talent, balance of, 82
Techniques
control, 84
expenditure on, 124–6
use in
purchasing, 38–9
stock control, 25
Technological change, 24, 27
food processing, 27
Technological forecasting, 27, 144–5
Test marketing, 121
Time and motion study, 50
Trade-offs, 159, 161
Trade unions, 36–7
Trades Descriptions Act 1967, 37
Training, *see* Marketing education

User domination of manufacturer, 39

Value analysis, 38, 39, 167
Ventures, 75
analysis, 27
group, 172

Warehousing, public, 26
Weights and Measures Departments, 37